Presented to Sir John Best-Shaw by the
Headmaster, Staff and Pupils of Stockport
Grammar School.

2ⁿᵈ January, 1987.

STOCKPORT GRAMMAR SCHOOL
1487–1987

STOCKPORT GRAMMAR SCHOOL
SCHOOL
1487–1987

by
James Ball, M.A., Ph.D. and William Ball, M.A.

Old Vicarage Publications
Congleton

Stockport Grammar School, 1487–1987
© 1987 J. G. & W. B. Ball

Printed by
Heffers Printers Limited,
King's Hedges Road,
Cambridge, CB4 2PQ.

First published 1987
by
Old Vicarage Publications,
The Old Vicarage,
Reades Lane,
Dane in Shaw,
Congleton, CW12 3LL.

Stockport Grammar School: 1487–1987.
  1. Stockport Grammar School – History
  I. Ball, James II. Ball, William
  373.427′34   LF695.S73/

  ISBN 0-947818-05-7
  ISBN 0-947818-06-5 Pbk
  ISBN 0-947818-04-9 Limited ed.

This work is dedicated to
THE WORSHIPFUL COMPANY OF GOLDSMITHS

PREFACE

Mr. Benjamin Varley's *History of Stockport Grammar School* first appeared in 1946, and there was a second enlarged edition in 1957. The debt which we owe to and the inspiration which we have drawn from that book are obvious, and are freely admitted. He was the pioneer, and had made the *History* his life's work; and he made our task that much easier. But he was working under enormous difficulties, which he mentions in his Prefaces: it was wartime, and the aftermath of wartime, when he was writing, and he was not well – indeed he suffered a heart attack whilst he was preparing the Second Edition in the archives of the Goldsmiths' Company in London in 1952.

We have written a new History for the Quincentenary, deliberately and consciously keeping largely to the story of the School, with only the occasional glance at the outside world. In general, James Ball is responsible for the period up to 1830, William Ball for the remainder, though each has often trodden the other's furrow. We have examined afresh all the primary material – such as it is – which Varley knew but sometimes did not use, for example, Hardwick's original drawings for the magnificent new School in Greek Street, in the Goldsmiths' archives. New material has also come to light, both in those same archives and at School, and we have been able to draw freely on this, thanks to the generosity of those involved.

In view of our predecessor's full and detailed treatment of the earlier part of the School's history, we have felt justified in being rather brief there, though we have not knowingly omitted anything of importance. The story of the past century has been one of almost incredible expansion—from the one teacher and 22 pupils of 1888 to the more than 80 and almost 1,000 of today—and our narrative has had to reflect that fact.

We have kept the 'history of the School a domestic story', as Professor Powicke noted in his Introduction to Varley's book, and for the same reasons:

'The materials are too scanty to . . . do more without affectation. The real and abiding strength of the School has lain and lies in the fact that it is the *Stockport* Grammar School; its strength is derived from the integrity and the devotion of its local sons.'

Thanks to our parents, we have both enjoyed the benefits of an education at Sir Edmond Shaa's school. As it enters its sixth century, we offer this book as a small token of our gratitude.

James Ball
Dulwich

William Ball
Congleton

1986

ACKNOWLEDGEMENTS

A book such as this owes its existence to many people. We should like especially to acknowledge the assistance of the following (in alphabetical order): J. H. Avery, J. Barnes, D. Beasley, W. D. Beckwith, D. R. J. Bird, D. B. Cassie, Dr. C. Challis, Miss A. A. Chamley, Lt. Col. J. A. Christie-Miller, J. G. Durnall, Mrs. M. Ellis, J. G. Gosling, Mrs. H. M. Greenwood, S. J. F. Harber, Miss S. M. Hare, N. G. Henshall, W. Herman, Wing Cdr. V. A. Hodgkinson, C. P. de B. Jenkins, W. A. Kershaw, Mrs. S. McKenna, F. J. Norris, R. D. H. Reeman, T. D. W. Reid, D. J. Roberts, H. D. Robinson, D. M. Scott, F. W. Scott, A. P. Smith, H. D. Smith, J. S. Southworth, J. T. Stanley, J. M. Swallow, J. B. Turner, A. L. Wilson, and H. R. Wright.

We thank also the librarians, archivists, researchers, and staff of Airviews (Manchester) Ltd., the British Library, the Goldsmiths' Company, the Guildhall Library, Manchester Central Library, the Mercers' Company, Millbrook House Ltd., the National Portrait Gallery, the National Westminster Bank, the John Rylands University Library of Manchester, Stockport Central Library, Stockport Grammar School, and Stockport Metropolitan Borough Council.

Publication of this book has been assisted by the generosity of the Sir Alan Sykes Trust, and all profits from the sale of the book will go towards entrance bursaries at the School.

The above, together with Mr. Varley and Sir Edmond Shaa, deserve the credit for this book; any errors which it contains we claim for ourselves.

JGB/WBB

CONTENTS

EXTRACT FROM THE WILL OF SIR EDMOND SHAA
20th March, 1487

AND I WOLL THAT THE OTHER HONEST PREEST

be a discrete man and conning in Gramer, and be able of conning to teche Grammer. I woll that he sing his masse and say his other divyne service in the Parisshe of Stopford, in the said Countie of Chestre. And to pray specially for my soule and the soules of my fader and moder. And I woll that the said connying Preest kepe a gram scole continually in the said Towne of Stopford and that he frely wtout any wagis or salarye asking or taking of any person, except only my salarye hereunder specified, shall teche allman persons children and other that woll com to hym to lerne, as well of the said Towne of Stopforde as of other Townes thereabout, the science of grammer as ferre as lieth in hym for to do in to the tyme that they be convenably instruct in gramer by hym after their capaciteys that God woll geve them.

Part of Sir Edmond's Will, transcribed in September 1979 by Mr. J. T. Stanley.

STOCKPORT

Stockport exists because of its rivers and rocks. From north and south in the foothills of the Pennines come the rivers Tame and Goyt, to unite here to form the Mersey, which flows through a deep gorge in a low ridge of sandstone, the westernmost ridge of those hills. The rivers, though not themselves navigable, provided an east–west route from Cheshire Plain to Pennines, and the ridge a north–south route. The routes cross at Stockport.

There is no conclusive proof, but it is a reasonable assumption, that the Romans knew the place, for it lies on the line of their road, which followed that ridge, between their settlements at Manchester and Buxton. It may be that there was a small

Two sections of Stockport's mediaeval Town Wall survive. One is behind 7, Mealhouse Brow; the other, behind 11 and 13 Great Underbank and seen here, incorporates a buttress and a gargoyle. [Reproduced by permission of the Metropolitan Borough of Stockport.]

military station to guard a river crossing, either a bridge or a ford, in the Tiviot Dale area. A coin of the Emperor Honorius (AD 393–423) is said to have been found during the demolition of the castle in the 18th century, but it has now been lost.

After the end of Roman rule, the picture is equally unclear. While there is no mention of Stockport in the Domesday Book, William the Conqueror had granted the County Palatine of Chester to Hugh Lupus, his nephew, and the town became one of his eight baronies, with a castle erected on a sandstone bluff (now Castle Yard) commanding the river crossing. It seems that whatever Saxon settlement there had been was so devastated during the Norman advance of 1070 that it was still uninhabited at the time of the survey in 1086.

Protected by the castle, a settlement grew up, apparently outside the bailey walls on the lower ground, with the modern market area seemingly remaining clear until the 16th century. What is certain is the founding of a church dedicated to St. Mary – there is a list of Rectors of this, the Parish Church of Stockport, going back to 1190. Also at this time, during the reign of Richard I (1189–1199), the de Stokeport family took over the Lordship of the Manor. A Charter making Stockport a free borough was granted by the Earl of Chester in about 1220; and a second Charter granted in 1260 gave the right to hold a market each Friday and an annual Fair, commencing on St. Wilfred's Day and running for the seven days following. By the end of the 14th century the Warren family of Poynton had become Lords of the Manor, a title which they were to retain until the death of Sir George Warren in 1801. He was succeeded by his daughter, and on her death in 1826 the Barony passed by will to Lady Vernon of Sudbury Hall in Derbyshire.

Of the structures of mediaeval Stockport, only two sections of the town walls (of rough dressed red sandstone) and the chancel of the Parish Church (in decorated Gothic) remain: the rest of the church was rebuilt early in the 19th century. The ordinary houses, of wattle and daub construction, have perished with the passage of time, though three interesting examples of slightly later work do survive – the National Westminster Bank building on Great Underbank, the Three Shires Restaurant on Chestergate, and the Staircase Café in the Market Place. This central area of the town – Hillgate, Millgate, the Underbanks, all names attested in the 15th century – does however retain both the mediaeval street plan and something of a mediaeval atmosphere, because of the narrow, twisting, hilly streets and the buildings crowding in on one another.[1]

12

Stockport

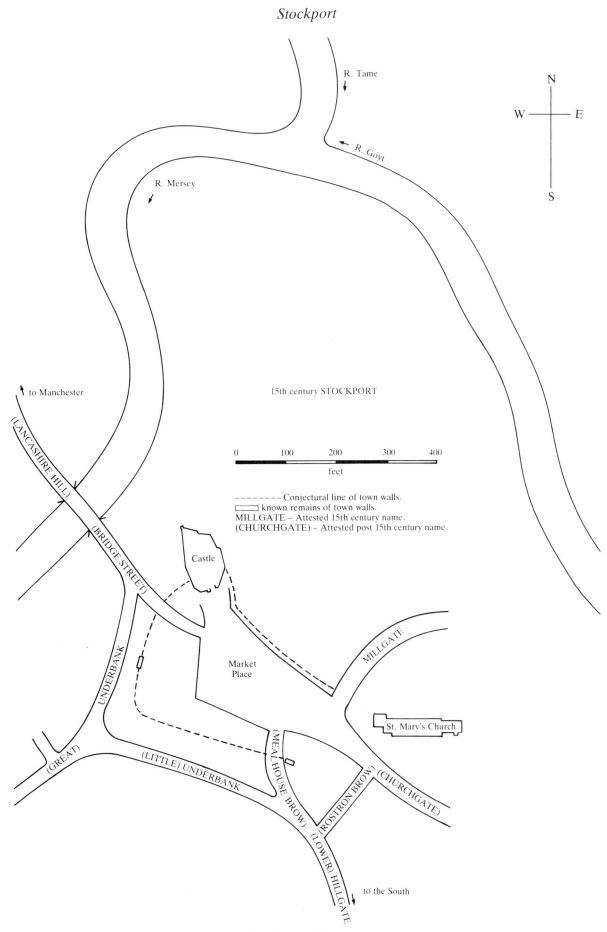

Stockport in the 15th century.

SHAA[1]

The other survivor from the Stockport of this time is the Grammar School, founded under the terms of the will of Sir Edmond Shaa, who died on 20th April 1488. His parents were from Dukinfield, which was then a hamlet in the parish of St. Mary, Stockport, where they were buried. The details of his early life are not known, but by 1450 he was apprenticed to Robert Botiller, a goldsmith in London, and by 1458 had become a lowys (the term used in the records of the Goldsmiths' Company to describe someone allowed to practise the craft). In 1462, under Edward IV, he received the life grant of the office of engraver to the Tower mint and all other mints in England and Calais, which he held for 20 years before relinquishing it in favour of his nephew, John Shaa. He was a Warden of the Goldsmiths' Company in 1467 and 1471, becoming Prime Warden in 1476. He served as Alderman for Cripplegate Ward from 1473 to 1485, and for Cheap from 1485 until his death. In 1474 he held the office of Sheriff of London and Middlesex, and was Mayor of London in 1482–83 – the 200th Mayor of the City, and the eleventh Goldsmith to hold the honour.[2]

His term as Mayor coincided with one of the most turbulent periods in English history. The facts are clear enough, but the details still arouse controversy today. The King, Edward IV, died on 9th April 1483, aged only 40, leaving as his successor his 12-year-old son, the prince Edward. The prince's guardian was his uncle, Richard, Duke of Gloucester. With due ceremony the Mayor and his entourage rode from London on 4th May to greet the new King, who was coming from Ludlow. On 19th May Edward moved into the Tower of London to await his Coronation, which had been set for 22nd June. His younger brother, Richard, Duke of York, joined him on 16th June. Supported by the Duke of Buckingham, Gloucester asserted that the two princes were illegitimate, and that he, as brother of Edward IV, was therefore the rightful king. In support of this proposition, Dr. Ralph Shaa, Edmond's brother and Prebendary of St. Paul's preached a sermon based on a text from the Book of Wisdom (4, 3), 'The ungodly shall not thrive, nor take deep rooting from bastard slips'. There was no great enthusiasm for Gloucester, but equally there was no great opposition to him, and Buckingham engineered the situation in such a way that on 25th

June Edmond as Mayor and other leading citizens offered the crown to Gloucester, who eventually accepted. The Princes in the Tower were not seen alive in public again and Gloucester became King Richard III.

Shortly after the coronation, which took place on 6th July, Edmond was knighted. During August he received a commission to attend the defences at the mouth of the Thames and an appointment as a Judge of Assize. During the remainder of Richard's short reign, Sir Edmond's career prospered: royal warrants and letters patent conferred further honours and duties upon him. A rebellion led by the disaffected Duke of Buckingham was

Edmond, Mayor of London, kneels to offer the crown to the Duke of Gloucester, the future Richard III.
[From a mural painting by Sigismund Goetze in the Royal Exchange in London: reproduced by permission of the Joint Grand Gresham Committee.]

This, the last Shaw Hall, at Church Coppenhall, was erected during the 1840s but demolished in 1939. It stood on the site of the ancient moated residence of the main Cheshire branch of the family.

He wrote at what turned out to be the end of an era. The Wars of the Roses had been brought to an end by the victory of Henry VII, and his dynasty was to last until 1603. Like many others, the Shaa brothers had, of course, played their part in the turbulent political troubles of London and England and were no strangers to the vicissitudes of human life. But Sir Edmond had survived and, surrounded by change, he saw continuity in God and in His Church. His will is an eloquent testimony of how conventional he was in his views – requiring Requiem Masses and prayers in perpetual memory of himself and of his family – and of how little he foresaw (for how could he?) the changes which were to affect the church – and his bequests – during the next century with the coming of the Reformation.

crushed with help from, amongst other, the Goldsmiths' Company: fifty-six of them were ordered each to raise between one and five others, in addition to 73 young men out of the livery.

Sir Edmond at this time lived in Foster Lane close to Goldsmiths' Hall. During 1484 he and his fellow goldsmith Thomas Wood paid for the insertion of a bay window bearing their arms in the eastern wall of the Hall. A further royal patent of May 1485 granted Sir Edmond a share of the Manor of Ockendon in Essex, lately forfeit to the king. But Richard's reign was soon to end. Henry Tudor, Earl of Richmond, landed at Milford Haven on 7th August and drew Richard to battle at Market Bosworth in Leicestershire.

The king was killed in the battle which was fought on 22nd August, and Richmond became Henry VII, the first of the Tudor kings. Within four months Sir Edmond had received a writ under the privy seal for the working of gold and silver for the new king; in the following year he, his nephew John Shaa, and his friend Sir Reginald Bray were granted possession of a large estate in Essex, augmenting earlier acquisitions. The last known civic function in which he took part was the election by the council of Sir William Horne as Mayor on 13th October 1487.[3]

Sir Edmond made his will on 20th March the following year, exactly a month before his death.

'In the name of God be it Amen, the xxthe day of the Monthe of Marche the yere of our Lorde after thaccompt of the Churche of Englond Mccccclxxxvijth and the iijde yere of the Reigne of King Henry the Vijth . . .'[4]

Sir Edmond is one of six benefactors commemorated by having their Arms displayed on the landing at Goldsmiths' Hall in London.
[Reproduced by permission of the Worshipful Company of Goldsmiths.]

SCHOOL AND CHAPEL[1]

He gave full instructions for the execution of various religious and charitable bequests, and in particular outlined the practical steps to be taken to found a school in Stockport. The common way to set up a school at this time was by means of a chantry. This was usually a small chapel, in or next to a church, endowed with funds to maintain one or more priests who would chant masses for the soul of the founder (or for some other person named by him). The founder often made provision for the mass-priest to teach a grammar school.

However, in accordance with the conventions of the time, and because of his anticipated death, much would remain for his executors to arrange. Sir Edmond intended that the bulk of the work should fall upon his 'right especial and tender loving friend' Sir Reginald Bray; the other four executors – Geoffrey Downes of Pott Shrigley; Thomas Rich, Mercer, his son-in-law; John Shaa, his nephew (but conventionally styled his 'cousin' in the will); and Julian, his wife – had the function of approving rather than initiating.

The execution of the will was certainly not a quick and easy process because of the number and geographical range of the bequests: there were the arrangements for his burial in the Church of St. Thomas of Acre in London, the founding of a

Sir Edmond's sole local executor was Geoffrey Downes of Pott Shrigley, who was also responsible for the enlargement and endowment of the village church in 1493. It contains some pre-Reformation glass, including a window dedicated, after God, to Lady Joan Ingoldesthorpe, who is affectionately remembered in the will.

Sir Edmond also founded a little chantry chapel at Woodhead in the Longdendale valley. The area can be only a little less bleak today than it was in the 15th century. The present building, dedicated to St. James, dates only from the last century; the porch is later, being a memorial of the Great War. In the churchyard are the graves of some of the navvies killed during the construction of the Woodhead tunnels of the Manchester, Sheffield, & Lincolnshire Railway. The first of these was dug between 1838 and 1845 at a cost of just over £200,000. At 3 miles 22 yards in length, it was at that time the longest in the world, and 26 men died during the work. A second tunnel, 6 feet longer than the first, was dug between 1848 and 1852. Cholera killed 28 during 1849. The Chairman of the MS & L, Sir Edward Watkin, was the School's Speech Day guest in December 1892.

chapel at Woodhead and the School in Stockport, together with masses and annual and daily services of prayers for his soul, road building in Essex, repair of the Cripplegate in London, gifts to the poor in and around Stockport and London and to churches in Stockport, Ashton, and Mottram, mourning rings to be made for particular friends, and legacies to his family.

Before there could be any school in Stockport, it was first necessary for the executors to purchase property which could then be legally transferred to the Goldsmiths' Company. This property, in Foster Lane, Bow Lane, and Watling Street, is first enumerated in a rent roll of Christmas 1496. It was intended to produce a secure annual income of £17, of which £10 was to be devoted to the salary of the schoolmaster-priest in Stockport and £4 6 8d to the priest at the chapel in Longdendale. This arrangement depended upon the Goldsmiths' willingness to undertake the task but the executors had the power, if the Company declined, to assign the property elsewhere. This actually happened in the case of Sir Edmond's chantry at St. Thomas of Acre, and in fact the Mercers' Company took on the responsibility. For administering the bequest, the Goldsmiths would receive the remaining £2 13 4d of the annual £17 and be required to have for ever 'the presentement, nominacion, and admyssyon' and 'the removing and puttyng out' of the priests in their care.

The Goldsmiths were not immediately willing to undertake the duties expected of them. Stockport was far from London and perhaps the burden of responsibility seemed to outweigh the £2 13 4d. At a meeting of the Company on 5th November 1491, called at the request of Thomas Rich in the name of Julian Shaa and the other executors, the Goldsmiths asked if they might have £40 clear: this would allow them to fulfil all their obligations, to have some money spare for repairs and suchlike, and also to appropriate the balance to their own use.

John Stanley

In his will, Sir Edmond ordered sixteen mourning rings to be made and distributed among his friends. Similar rings have been discovered in Coventry in 1803 and Hackney in 1895. The former, now preserved in the British Museum, was described in the Gentleman's Magazine in June 1803. The five wounds of Jesus, on the outside of the ring, are compared with five wells of sacred gifts. Within the ring are engraved the words:

> *Vulnera quinqu' Dei sunt medicina mei pia.*
> *Crus et passis X'pi sunt medicina michi.*
> *Jaspar, Melchior et Baltazar.*
> *Avanyzapta, tetragrammaton.*

The first three lines are a mixture of Greek (X'pι) and Latin: 'The five wounds of God are my beloved medicine. The cross and suffering of Christ are my cure. Jaspar, Melchior, and Baltazar' [the Three Wise Men]. Avanyzapta could be a mediaeval equivalent of 'abracadabra'. Tetragrammaton is Greek again, meaning 'of four letters' – especially the four with which the Hebrews, omitting the vowels, spelled the name JeHoVaH.

There were various conditions attached to the will. The Goldsmiths were bound to attend Sir Edmond's obit [anniversary service] every year. For this the four Wardens of the Company would receive 3s 4d each; there was also a 'potation' which was to be held on the preceding evening (at a cost of 12s 6d) and after the service there was a dinner (15s 6d); finally, twelve poor members of the Goldsmiths' Company were to be given a shilling each.[2]

All these obligations were accounted for in the first recorded reference to the properties in the Company's books on 19th April 1496 together with the £10 for John Randall, the school's first known Master, and the £4 6 8d to John Bockley, the priest at Longdendale. However, the total income from rent was a gross £36 6 0d; from that had to be deducted a quit rent of 13s 4d to St. Bartholomew's Hospital, leaving £18 12 8d (after the other deductions) to be appropriated by the Company. The eventual income rose to £40 6 0d on the accession of certain additional property in Wood Street by Sir John Shaa.[3]

Not until 1495 were all the conditions of Sir Edmond's will fulfilled. Only then were Geoffrey Downes and John Shaa able to go to the Chancery at Winchester on 6th July; not until 1506 would the Goldsmiths physically possess the income from which the School was to be supported, when Thomas Fereby transferred the deeds of the property to the Company.

These early years of Sir Edmond's foundations in the north are obscure. Bockley had served over 23 years at the chapel in Longdendale when he died in 1519. On 28th July his successor, Hugh Silvester, was appointed. Although the chapel was not even mentioned in the commission of 1535, the foundation certainly continued: its third incumbent, Thomas Hattfield, was installed on 1st July 1541 after Silvester's death. The Goldsmiths, however, had little certain knowledge of the place. In fact, there is no further mention of the chapel in the Minute Books of their Meetings for nearly three centuries, and much later they were to claim that they did not know about it until it was brought to their attention for the first time in 1846. However, there appears no doubt that the stipend was officially paid throughout this period.[4]

The name of the first recorded Master of the school in Stockport is John Randall. When he was appointed is not known, but it was before 1496, for the rent roll dated Christmas of that year shows payment of £10 to him as priest and Schoolmaster at Stockport. There is no reason for the School not to have been in operation very soon after Sir Edmond's death. Not even a special building was required, for since the Master was, as required by the will, a priest in Holy Orders singing masses for his patron at an altar in the Parish Church, it is entirely conceivable that the School's first home was somewhere in that Church. Examples of such usage from elsewhere are common; certainly in 1536 William Chorleton was both master of the School and the priest serving the Lady Chapel at St. Mary's in Stockport.

The Davenport Chapel at St. Mary's Parish Church in Stockport may have been the earliest home of the School. Sir Edmond's will stipulated:
'I woll that the preest sing his masse and say his other divyne service in the Parisshe of Stopford . . . and kepe a gram scole continually in the said Towne.'
It is known that William Chorleton, Master in the 16th century, served this chapel, dedicated to St. Mary.

School and Chapel

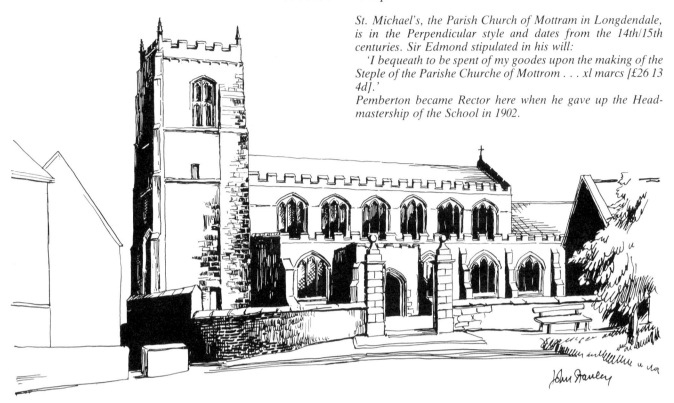

St. Michael's, the Parish Church of Mottram in Longdendale, is in the Perpendicular style and dates from the 14th/15th centuries. Sir Edmond stipulated in his will:

'I bequeath to be spent of my goodes upon the making of the Steple of the Parishe Churche of Mottrom . . . xl marcs [£26 13 4d].'

Pemberton became Rector here when he gave up the Head-mastership of the School in 1902.

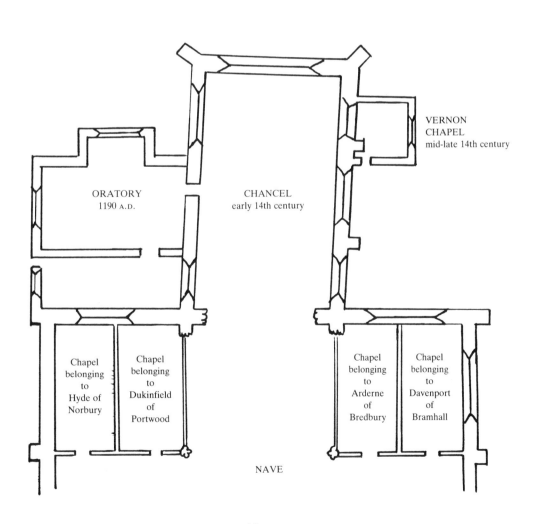

ORATORY
1190 A.D.

CHANCEL
early 14th century

VERNON CHAPEL
mid-late 14th century

Chapel belonging to Hyde of Norbury

Chapel belonging to Dukinfield of Portwood

Chapel belonging to Arderne of Bredbury

Chapel belonging to Davenport of Bramhall

NAVE

THE 16th CENTURY

The Master's duties fell into two areas: he had to teach 'the science of grammar' – effectively Latin – and also, every Wednesday and Friday, to pray in St. Mary's Church for the souls of the founder's mother and father. He and all the scholars in company were there to 'say together Psalm 130 *De Profundis* with the versicles and collect thereto accustomed after Salisbury use'.[1]

Although the practice has now become annual instead of twice weekly – at the revived Founder's Day Service, held in St. Mary's Church – the Latin psalm is still sung. This remains part of the School's tradition and is recognisable after five hundred years. The system of education, however, was quite different.

In the fifteenth and sixteenth centuries 'grammar' meant Latin grammar. According to William Wykeham, in the foundation charter of his College at Winchester, it was 'the foundation, gate and source of all the other liberal arts.' The basic text book would have been something like Lily's Latin Grammar, which, in the revised edition by Leonard Cox, was made official in England during the 1540s. Indeed, even in the eighteenth century, the Master's job was still formally described as 'teaching Lillye Grammer'. There was as yet no separate building (other than St. Mary's) and much must have depended on the enthusiasm – and ability – of the priest. His pupils might already have attended a reading or song school. But it is probable – at least in a small town such as Stockport – that the School represented their first experience of being taught. The boys had no fees to pay – for Sir Edmond had stipulated in the will that all scholastic instruction should be free – and they would continue to live at home with their parents. Therefore, they would not have to meet any boarding expenses.

Although the Master was not allowed any wages or salary for his teaching beyond the £10 specified in the bequest, he was not prevented from taking other paid duties to supplement his income, perhaps for example serving a local family in its chapel. But in this period his salary, although not extravagant, was generous enough: the priest at Longdendale was allocated less than half the Master's £10, which stood at the higher level of salaries, ranging from £4 6 0d to £12 6 0d, at this time for such a position. The education of the Master himself would probably have been gained at a grammar school of a similar sort.

These early years of the sixteenth century saw the flourishing of 'the new learning'. Tudor England was no cultured and sophisticated Italian state, but the country did feel the influence of the humanists and gave hospitality to Erasmus. The ancient Universities and the capital were the centres of education – the famous school of St. Paul's was founded in 1509 – but the north west of England too felt the impetus of new ideas. Macclesfield's Grammar School was founded in 1502, Manchester's in 1515, and Bolton's in 1524. Chester, a flourishing county town, had the King's School founded in 1541.

Sir Edmond had been the first of the Goldsmiths to found a School but his example was soon followed. In his will of 19th October 1505, Sir Bartholomew Read left property to the Company to support a school in Cromer. As in Stockport, the Master's salary was fixed at £10 but Read included far more details for religious exercises and attendances. He also involved a religious foundation – the Charterhouse – in his scheme (although it appears that in practice it played little part) and wanted his Master to be a Scholar of Eton or of Winchester (if such could be found) and to be appointed on the recommendation of the Provosts of Eton College and of King's College, Cambridge.[2]

Although Read's will was far more detailed than Sir Edmond's, the circumstances surrounding its execution are rather more obscure; certainly little

The Three Shires Restaurant.

notice appears to have been taken of the complicated procedure for appointment. One early candidate, Henry Plough in 1517, was simply appointed; the opinion of the local priest – and, one assumes, of the local community – must have played a large part in most recommendations. The Goldsmiths' Company may also have paid attention to other claims upon them. John Lee – possibly one of the candidates for Stockport's School in 1534 (he was born in Baguley, three miles from Stockport) – was appointed Master at Cromer on 27th October 1534. He did, however, have a testimonial from the Master of Charterhouse. John Harlow, appointed in 1560, was himself the local vicar and his candidature was approved by the parishioners; when the Goldsmiths examined him, they declared themselves satisfied without noting his qualifications and without recourse to external referees. In Stockport too there were new Masters. Randall Hulton had arrived before 1509 and served until 1521. He was succeeded by George Bamford who was appointed on 17th September 1521 and stayed in office until 1533.

By the end of the reign of Henry VIII in January 1547 the structure of the English state had changed fundamentally. The King had moved from being 'Defender of the Faith' – a title bestowed by the Pope in Rome in 1521 – to become the dissolver of the monasteries. The expansion of learning, which had started in the second half of the fifteenth century, now began to attract Royal attention. In 1536 all clergy were required to instruct the young and in 1538 priests had to expound the English Bible. It was a time of rapid and revolutionary change, in which the schools were closely involved. The old theology was still largely intact but in one respect – in the doctrine of Purgatory – an attack was made on the theory and on the theological basis of the chantries which inevitably affected their co-foundations, the schools.

Purgatory, according to Roman Catholic faith, was a state of suffering after death in which the souls of those who died in venial sin, and of those who still owed some debt of temporal punishment for mortal sin, were rendered fit for heaven. The passage of the soul onward from Purgatory was effected by the prayers of the living for the dead, and in particular by the masses offered by the chantry priests.

The first Act to abolish Chantries, in 1545, had lapsed before it could take effect. Edward VI's Bill of 1547 encountered a great deal of opposition throughout English society not only because it concerned the chantries but also because it struck at the system of confraternities on which much of mediaeval life was based. For, as we have seen, intermixed with the foundations of perpetual

The National Westminster Bank's premises at 10, Great Underbank, recently extensively and expensively renovated, were once the Underbank Hall of the Ardern family. The building has been a bank since 1824, when William Miller Christy and John Worsley (both hat manufacturers), Isaac Lloyd (of the Birmingham banking family), and John K. Winterbottom opened Christy, Lloyd & Co. for business. Miller Christy was an ancestor of Colonel Sir Geoffry Christie-Miller; Winterbottom, Lady Vernon's Steward, was the Bank's solicitor. In 1829 the Manchester & Liverpool District Banking Co. Ltd. (later the District Bank) took over the premises for £4,150. In 1840 Winterbottom, owing the Bank £35,000, fled the country and went to France. He returned to England in 1844, was tried, and found guilty. He was sentenced to transportation to Botany Bay, in spite of a petition said to have been 62 yards long and containing 20,000 signatures. (As the population of Stockport was recorded as 28,419 in 1841, this implies that every adult in the town signed the document!) His wife accompanied him, and after his release he became Town Clerk of Hobart in Tasmania. Unfortunately he committed further crimes and eventually died in prison.

The School has banked here since 1866, when the then Manager, Mr. Rhind was appointed its Treasurer. The tradition continues today, and the present manager of the Bank, Mr. J. Barnes, has been a Governor of the School since 1979.

Both this building and the Three Shires Restaurant date from the 16th century and are of typical timber-framed construction.

prayers – which in the Act were now declared to be 'superstitious' – were the educational foundations.[3]

The famous English institutions of learning, the universities and colleges of Oxford and Cambridge and the colleges at Eton and Winchester were specifically exempted from the provisions of the Act, as they had been from earlier legislation. But all the endowments which funded chantries were confiscated at Easter 1548 and vested in the Crown. The continuity of education should, however, have been assured by the requirement that former chantry priests – now pensioners dependent on the Court of Augmentations – were to teach the English Bible which was now widely available to the population.[4]

But the less well known foundations were threatened with extinction and many did not survive in their old state: some were refounded (King's School in Macclesfield, for example, received generous new endowments) but not all benefited. Although it was decided after all to allow the continuation of school foundations, in many cases the continuity had already been lost; and by 1550, when the Court of Augmentations began to fund such foundations, the theory of English educational endowment had entered a new era.

The Grammar School in Stockport, however, avoided the extinction which other schools had suffered, for during this turbulent period it was itself in a sort of Limbo. On 15th February 1544, a year before the passing of the first Act, the official Master, William Chorleton, applied for leave. He was a local man, 'born within ii myles of Stopporte', and had been appointed by the Goldsmiths on 28th October 1534. Supported by the local community, he had probably been selected by them, for his appointment by the Company included a note that he had been teaching since Michaelmas 1533. He asked that a deputy be appointed for his teaching duties while he himself left to pursue an ecclesiastical career in the newly created Diocese of Chester.

It may be that he was one of the many unlearned priests forced to absent themselves for the sake of their own education, but his going to Chester seems to suggest rather that he was both able and ambitious in the new province. Certainly Chester, which was the successor to the Diocese of Lichfield as the ecclesiastical authority for Stockport, offered great opportunities.

Chorleton's replacement, about whom little, not even his name, is known, suffered as the first Master to be subjected to the complaints of the local community, expressed formally to the Goldsmiths by William Davenport of Bramhall in April 1545. The exact details of the complaint are not recorded, but they were taken seriously enough by the Goldsmiths, who summoned the deputy to London to explain his conduct to them in person. At a meeting on 25th September they accepted his explanation and sent him back to Stockport, where he apparently continued his work for a total of thirteen years, until Chorleton returned to take up his position. The Goldsmiths confirmed Chorleton's re-appointment formally on 19th May 1557, when they acknowledged that he had actually been in office since the previous Lady Day. This back-dating of the appointment was not of significance at the time but it is an early example of how masters in Stockport could come and go without the immediate supervision of the Company. It was also in this year that the Company lost – at least legally – its sole right of control over appointments, for schoolmasters were now required to hold licences from the Bishop of their province – in this case, Chester.[5]

The School had thus survived the Reformation with its continuity unbroken. Several reasons can plausibly be suggested for this: the distance of Stockport from London, the ineffectiveness of the local officers of the Court of Augmentations, confusions of jurisdiction, or simply the relative insignificance of the small town.[6]

As a London Livery Company, however, the Goldsmiths did not escape the notice of the authorities. After the Dissolution of the Monasteries, the Goldsmiths had in 1538 already sued in the Court of Augmentations for the wills and bequests of Sir Edmond and Sir Bartholomew Read. They supported a considerable number of genuine charities as well as the disputable School, and were particularly affected by the new legislation of 1547. The total capital value of the property lost by the thirty three Companies of the city amounted to over £18,000. In 1550 three London gentlemen paid £18,744 11 2d, which entitled them to an annual income of £939 2 5½d from the various properties. In 1548 the Goldsmiths had calculated their liability at £103 17 8d; in the event, they lost rentals worth £107 16 9d annually in 1550, together with a further 8s 0d the following year. This meant a loss of income of around one fifth for the Goldsmiths. In a subsidy assessment of 1554 they estimated their annual income at over £500: of this some £360 was expended on various charities (including the salaries of 'divers schoolmasters').

There is no mention of Sir Edmond or Stockport in the patent roll of 1550, but the properties transferred by Thomas Fereby ('messuages in the parishes of St. John Zachary, St. Michael in Woodstrete, St. Mary at Bowe and St. Mary de Aldermary') do appear, valued at £2 13 4d, and described as 'for the anniversary of Thomas Ferrebe in the Church of St. John Zachary'; the figure corresponds with the total of Sir Edmond's obit (£2 1 4d) and the gift to the poor of 12s 0d. Fereby was the trustee empowered to administer the estate supporting both the School and the chapel at Woodhead; the properties were listed in full in his will of 28th July 1506, and transferred to the Company by a deed of 6th August the same year. The School itself therefore continued without a break, as the income from the property which had been devised to support it was thus not forfeit.[7]

William Chorleton had returned to spend his last two years at the School. On 21st April 1559 his death was reported to the Company, and a replacement, Leonard Harrison, was appointed on 12th June and served until about 1564. There then came three Masters in quick succession, Thomas Leigh, John Brownswerd, and Richard Heywood. Leigh, who drew a quarter's salary in March 1565, was another graduate of the University of Cambridge; good boys from the School were going on to University. Such success was not, however, reflected in the Master's salary, which in a period of notable inflation remained at £10. Moreover his duties had become more onerous for he was now teaching – still free of charge as the Founder's will required – pupils from outside the area of the 'towne of Stopforde [and] of other Townes thereabout' which had originally been stipulated.

Brownswerd was recommended to the Master's post while Leigh was still in office, and his appointment was confirmed on 29th March 1565; he had taught already in Wilmslow and Macclesfield, and was to teach later at Stratford-on-Avon and again at Macclesfield, where he died on 15th April 1589. However long he was at Stockport – and it was not long – he is its only Master to be recorded (as a poet) in the Dictionary of National Biography.

Heywood was another local recommendation, being appointed first on 21st May 1565 only temporarily, 'till Mr. Brownswerd or some other learned man may be gotte'. In 1568 comment was made to the Goldsmiths by Mr. Francis Elcock, a local worthy, that £10 'seemeth a very scant living' but the hint was not taken; a decade later, formal permission was asked of the Company to charge fees, but it was refused. At least to the Goldsmiths, £10 seemed adequate: as late as 1597, when John Fox founded a free Grammar School at Deane in Cumberland after the examples of Stockport and Cromer, the Master's salary was fixed at the same £10.

Heywood's successor was called Bamford, but we do not know his Christian name. Three of his pupils – William Nicholson, Thomas Thornely, and John Lowe – went on to Caius College at Cambridge, a connection no doubt brought about by the Rector of Stockport at this time, Richard Gerard, a Fellow of Caius and Chaplain to Elizabeth I. Nicholson was from Reddish, but the others came from farther afield: Thornely from Denton, and Lowe from Haughton, both in Lancashire.

The next master was Francis Lowe, the first such to be recorded in the Stockport Parish Registers. He was buried on 29th December, 1587, having died possible of the plague, which struck Stockport between 1587 and 1592.

The Masters at Stockport faced a problem with regard to their salary. For them as clergymen the obvious solution was to take on other duties to supplement the £10, but administratively it was clearly better that they should be paid, adequately, for their work without being forced to divert their energies in other directions. Since Sir Edmond's will ruled out charging fees, there were two possible solutions: either the Goldsmiths would have to increase the stipend from their own income from Shaa's bequest, or the local community would have to take a hand. This would mean, of course, that the town would begin to exert not only an influence but a direct effective power over the School by subsidising the Master's salary.

Towards the end of the sixteenth century, the trend to the latter solution became apparent. The gentlemen of the town were supplementing the stipend, and the next Master, William Nicholson, gave the sum of £10 in his will of 1597 to pay an Usher to be an assistant, and another £10 for the same purpose came in 1605 under the will of Alexander Torkington. Nicholson, the earliest known pupil of the School, had proceeded to Caius College, Cambridge in 1581, but graduated from St. John's College in 1584–5 and took his MA in 1588. The Parish Registers record his burial on 5th September 1597, and both they and his will testify to his having been the Master. At his death he was owed £5 in salary from the Goldsmiths (which was paid through the Mayor, then Alexander Lowe) and £14 in 'Schole wages', the local subsidy. This latter amount he left to the five daughters of Edward Warren, Lord of the Manor. He also bequeathed to the School 'a greeke Scapula, a Cowpers dictionarie, my Hebrew Bible, and a little dictionarie in Hebrew'.

THE 17th CENTURY[1]

Despite the local subsidy, relations between School and Company remained cordial. In 1595 the Goldsmiths presented to Alexander Lowe a silver seal with an ivory handle to be kept in the custody of the Mayor; Lowe himself was another benefactor of the School. But the first controversy over appointments between the prestigious London Company, responsible for so many things, and the obscure community 180 difficult miles away occurred in 1601. On Nicholson's death William Lingard was appointed Master, and on 3rd April 1601 a Mr. Kirke succeeded him. Kirke did not stay long, for on 25th September the Goldsmiths appointed a Mr. Lang, recommended by the Mayor, Aldermen, and Townspeople. However the local Rector and gentry, together with the Bishop of Chester, applied on 12th October for his removal; the Goldsmiths complied, paid £5 to a Mr. Nicholson who had taught at the School in the meanwhile, and made John Cobb the new Master on 8th January 1602. Matters unfortunately did not improve. In June 1603 Cobb asked the Company for

'some allowance in respect of his charges in finding himself a scholehouse, for that the comon scholehouse was by the Mayor and townsmen of Stockport deteyned from him . . .'

His request shows that the School was no longer housed at the Parish Church, but unfortunately its whereabouts are not known. On 22nd July 1603 Cobb resigned, and on 20th February and 3rd July the following year the people of Stockport suggested Thomas Bower as the new Master. The Goldsmiths summoned him to London, but did not refer to his local supporters, appointing him on 7th August because of his excellent testimonials from the Master and Fellows of Christ's College, Cambridge, where he had been a student.

On 19th February 1607 the Goldsmiths met to consider unrecorded complaints against Bower from the townspeople. Nothing was resolved then, but in April the Company asked Sir Nicholas Moseley, Sir Peter Legh, Sir Urian Legh, and a Mr. Holland of Denton to investigate the charges. These four decided against the Master, but he appealed to the ecclesiastical authority of the Bishop of Chester. The Goldsmiths conferred with the Bishop, and Bower was eventually dismissed two years later.

Thanks to the generosity of Alexander Lowe the School soon gained a permanent home in Chestergate. In his will, dated 26th February 1608, he left

'the Under Roome of the howse wherein the Schoole ys nowe kepte to and for the use of the Schoole to be kepte theere for ever. The Scholmaster thereof for the tyme beinge yelding and paying yearely unto my heires and some of Sixe shillings Eight pence Rente.'

He also augmented the Master's salary:

'Item whereas there is Sixscore pounds due unto mee by Roger Harper and Johnn Barrett Payable at Certen Dayes and tymes agreed uponn betweene us, My mynde and will ys That the Somme of Fortye pounds being a Thirdd parte of the sayd Sixscore pounds shall be and remayne to the augmentacion and increase of the wages of the Schoolemaster of Stockport for the tyme beinge, for ever, to be hadd and receaved at suche dayes and tymes as the same shall bee due, And further I do will and bequeath the sume of Tenn pounds for and towards the augmenting of the Schoolmasters wages afforesayd to make upp the sayd sume of Fortye pounds the Full sume of Fyftie pounds All the sayd Sume to be Imployed and used for the benefit of the Schoolemaster afforesayde by the Parsonn of Stockporte the Maior of Stockport and the most Auncyent Alderman thereof for the time being.'

This was not all:

'And for the residue of my Thirdd parte of goods Remayning unbequeathed be yt moore or lesse My will and mynde ys that it shall remayne and bee for and towards the maynetenance of an usher to teache under the Scholemaster of Stockport for ever.'

Continuity was once more assured in a changing world and the School survived. The Master had not.

After Bower's eventual dismissal, a new Master, Luke Mason, was appointed on 8th April 1609. It is likely that Mason, who did not receive his degree from Emmanuel College, Cambridge, until later, took the post as a temporary position before embarking on an ecclesiastical career.

Mason resigned the following year, and on 7th October the Goldsmiths heard that 'Walter Pott was commended by the Inhabitants of Stockport in place of Luke Mason'. On the last day of the month the Company confirmed his appointment, subject only to his presenting himself in London. He did so, and continued in Stockport until 1623, being succeeded on 4th November by Thomas Rossen, who resigned within two years. To replace Rossen, Sir Urian Legh of Adlington recommended Reginald Pott, probably a relative of Walter and probably (with Walter) a member of the Pott family of Pott Shrigley, whose lands adjoined the Leghs'. Pott also resigned quite quickly, and Edmund Clough, a Cambridge graduate, took his place on 7th February 1628. Unfortunately within eight months he was dead, being buried at the Parish Church on 1st October.

The next Master was the youngest ever. John Pollett of Prestwich, Lancashire, having entered Brasenose College in October 1626 and graduated in October 1627, became Master on 7th August 1628 when only 19. But Pollett too did not stay long, for by April 1630 the townspeople had notified the Goldsmiths that William Plant was now 'teaching the children'. As the people of Stockport were taking care of the repairs to the School and contributing to the Master's salary, they requested permission to appoint a new man without the formality of an interview before the Company in London, which would necessitate an expensive and inconvenient journey. The Goldsmiths were not insensible of the problem; but instead of dispensing with the formality they offered the candidate as compensation thirty shillings – for a journey to London, the equivalent of 15% of the annual salary!

That salary was more than ever a disincentive: it seemed difficult to attract experienced candidates. Young graduates, like Mason and possibly Pollett, might take the position for a short time and then move on to better posts. The Company might not even hear of a replacement until he had been 'appointed' – unofficially, of course, by the local authorities, who continued to complain about the inadequate salary. The problem of supervision was not limited to Stockport: in 1652 the Goldsmiths were still regularly paying Read's £10 to the school in Cromer, but they had no idea whether it was still a Grammar School.

Plant's successor was Samuel Edwards, an Oxford graduate, appointed by the Company on 24th July 1633. He lasted only three or four months, for on 4th July 1634 Bradley Hayhurst appeared before the Goldsmiths, reporting that

'for these ¾ of a year no past he had taught the scholars of the school to the content of the inhabitants, who have sent their approbation and who desire him to be established therein.'

He was officially appointed on the following day, and served as Master until Christmas 1644. In the previous May Prince Rupert had captured the town for the Royalists from Colonel Dukinfield, who had held it for the Parliamentarians. In September Hayhurst wrote to the Goldsmiths to complain that his salary was several quarters in arrear.

Because of the difficulties caused by the Civil War, the next two Masters were appointed by the people of Stockport without reference to the Goldsmiths, who were naturally displeased. Randall Yarwood was eventually confirmed in the office by the Company on probation on 8th August 1645, but lasted only until Good Friday of the following year. A replacement, Thomas Peirson, was not found until Christmas, and he was not appointed formally by the Company until 17th September 1647, when the Mayor and Alderman had apologised.

King Charles I was executed on 30th January 1649. His death-warrant bore 58 signatures, headed by that of John Bradshaw who, born in Marple in 1602, may have attended the School in his youth; however, if he did, it seems to have made but little impression on him, for in his will he made bequests to increase the Masters' salaries at his other schools, Bunbury and Middleton, and to found a new school in Marple, without mentioning Stockport. In the event it made no difference: his property was confiscated under the Act of Attainder.[2]

In 1654, only a year after Cromwell had taken the title of Lord Protector of the Commonwealth, the School was the stage for the preaching of the independent divine, Samuel Eaton, a remarkable orator, whose speeches against the Book of Common Prayer were said to be so powerful that his listeners would refuse to go to Church. He had previously been a teacher at the Congregational Church in Dukinfield and was an assistant to the Parliamentary Commissioners of Stockport.

Meanwhile, the School had gained a new Master. Peirson had resigned on 1st February 1651, and there were two candidates for the post, William Duncan and Thomas Coombes. The latter, supported by a petition signed by the Mayor, Francis Harpur, and 120 others, and by a statement from the Rector, Thomas Johnson, that he was 'fit and able to teach a Grammar School', was appointed by the Goldsmiths on 9th April 1651. Duncan, a Cambridge graduate, had also been a candidate for the post when Peirson had been appointed in 1647, but the Company, anxious to avoid any trouble and to be reconciled with the townspeople, had on both occasions chosen Stockport's nominee.

After 17 successful years Coombes resigned in June 1668. The choice of his successor was not so easy, for this time there were two candidates from the town – Daniel Leech, who on 1st July

'presented alsoe a certificate subscribed by Divers of the inhabitants of the said Towne to the number of 62 persons . . . '

and John Steele,

'subscribed by the Maior of Stockport and some Aldermen and others about 12 in number.'

Leech, a member of an old Cheshire family, was appointed, but by September the Company had received

'a petition subscribed by 100 inhabitants of Stockport on behalf of Daniel Leech to be re-admitted to the schoolmaster's place, whereof he was in possession, but by indirect ways he was thence unduly ejected.'

The Goldsmiths confirmed the appointment in writing in October, but in December John Warren, Lord of the Manor, travelled to London to inform them that Leech was simply not competent. By the time the Master himself arrived in London to be examined in August 1669, he had already been suspended for two months past by the Chancellor of the Archbishop of York until the controversy could be settled. By the Act of Uniformity of 1662 the Chancellor had the right to suspend the schoolmaster on religious grounds, but it was no business of his whom the Company should appoint. Sir Edmond's will was quite clear:

'I woll that the said Felliship shall have for evermore the presentement, nominacion, and admyssyon of the said two Preestes of the said two services and the removing and puttyng out of them . . . '

Leech was examined on 18th August 1669 to see if he was able 'to instruct the youth so far as to fit them for the universities' by a panel composed of Dr. Slater, Mr. Watson (Schoolmaster of Sutton's Hospital), Mr. Holmes (Schoolmaster of Christ's Hospital), and Mr. Crumland (a master from St. Paul's). The Master was found lacking, and was dismissed by the Company on 1st September, with £10 compensation.

Hoping as always to avoid trouble, the Goldsmiths decided to require the new Schoolmaster to be examined before being appointed; this was duly done, and Joseph Whittle, a graduate of Brasenose College, Oxford, took up his position with effect from 28th September. He was given £2 10 0d to travel to Stockport. After four years at the School, he resigned with effect from Christmas 1673 to enter the Ministry full-time.

On 6th March 1674 Thomas Morris and Samuel Needham appeared before the Goldsmiths as the next candidates. Needham, who had attended the School under Coombes and later graduated from St. John's College, Cambridge in 1674–5, brought with him from Stockport a petition of 42 names (including the Mayor), and was duly appointed. He was a most successful Master, sending at least eleven boys on to Cambridge alone during his nine years in office. He was assisted in his work from time to time by Samuel Holmes, a graduate of Magdalene College, Cambridge, who hoped to succeed him, but in fact on 27th July 1683 Timothy Dobson, of Jesus College, Cambridge, was appointed. Needham had previously become Rector of Claughton in Lancashire, and because he could not be both Rector there and Master in Stockport simultaneously the Goldsmiths had required him to resign from the School.

Just as English society had changed since the foundation of the School, so had the curriculum. The 'science of grammar' was no longer simply Latin. From the early days, the children destined for university would have acquired at least the rudiments of Greek and perhaps even a little Hebrew: books in all three languages had been left to the School by William Nicholson, the Master, in 1597. The Christian religion was naturally of the greatest importance – the Master was in Holy Orders – but the Latin Vulgate had been replaced by the English of King James's Bible. Ovid and Seneca would have been the favourite Classical authors, and the children would study also reading and writing (in English) and arithmetic. As always, much depended upon the ability and enthusiasm of the Master, and in this respect the School seems generally to have been fortunate.

Dobson was responsible for the early education of the Shippen brothers. Their father, Dr. William Shippen (1635–1693) was a native of Stockport who enjoyed a varied ecclesiastical career, returning to his home town in 1678 to become Rector: his younger brother, Edward, first Mayor of Philadelphia in the then American colonies, is perhaps better remembered as the founder of the wealthy transatlantic branch of the family. William's second and eponymous son was educated at the School before transferring to Westminster and thence to Cambridge and a career in politics as leader of the Jacobite squires in the House of Commons; his younger brother, Robert, went directly from School to Merton College, Oxford, and there pursued an academic career, becoming Vice Chancellor of that University. The eldest brother, Edward, left School and went on to Brasenose College, Oxford, and became in time both an eminent physician and Professor of Music at Gresham College. The youngest of the family, John, was quite unlike his brothers and became a Spanish Merchant. None of the four returned to Stockport.

On 6th November 1689 Dobson was appointed Schoolmaster of Macclesfield (at a salary of £60 a year), but a faction of the Governors there installed Caleb Pott instead. Pott soon died, however, and Dobson was eventually reappointed on 14th June 1694, but as from the original date. Meanwhile, it seems that there had been two successors in Stockport. First George Escolmbe, an Oxford graduate, had been appointed on 14th September 1691, and then on 20th January 1693 the Goldsmiths 'unanimously agreed that William Dickens shall be appointed schoolmaster of the said town in the room of Timothy Dobson'. Since it took so long for Dobson finally to take over in Macclesfield, it may be either that he returned to Stockport as Master from some period or that the Goldsmiths forgot that they had appointed Escolmbe, or that Escolmbe himself never took up his duties.

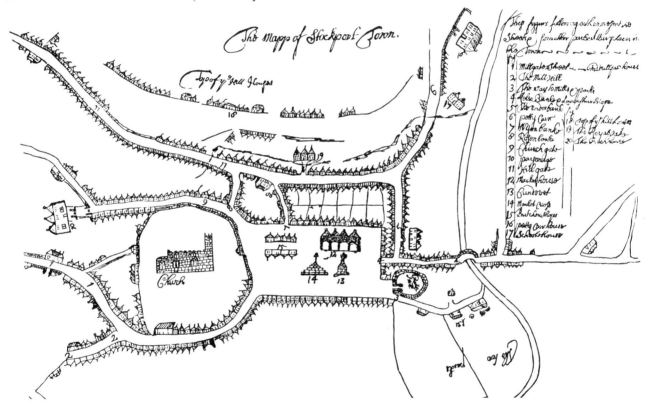

This early map of Stockport dates from about 1680 and shows the Chestergate site of the School (no. 17). It is not known when the School opened here, but it was before 1608, for the will of Alexander Lowe, a mercer and several times Mayor of Stockport who died in that year, contains the following:

'Item. I gyve and bequeathe the Under Roome of the howse wherein the Schoole ys nowe kepte to and for the use of the Schoole to be kepte theere for ever.'

Stockport in the 17th century was one of 13 market towns in Cheshire, but seems not to have had any large-scale industry, unlike Macclesfield with its buttons, Congleton with its leather, and of course the salt towns to the west. But Stockport linen, produced in the farmhouses and cottages of the area, was being sold in London as early as 1610. According to the hearth tax return of 1664 the township of Stockport contained just over 1,300 people in 289 households. Just over 100 years later, Daniel Defoe in his 'Tour' described Stockport as

'A large and handsome town . . . inhabited by a great number of gentry and well filled with warehousemen who carry on the check, mohair, button, and hat manufactures. Here the raw silk is chiefly thrown and prepared for the Spitalfields weavers by six engines the buildings of which are of prodigious bulk, one of them containing above 45,000 movements which fill the spacious room up to the fifth storey and are all put in motion by one wheel that goes by water. Poverty is not much felt except by those who are idle.'

Even after the introduction of mills powered by water and steam, the 'domestic' industries continued to thrive until the beginning of the 19th century, and at the time of the first Census in 1801 Stockport's population had reached 14,830.

[Reproduced by permission of the Metropolitan Borough of Stockport.]

THE 18th CENTURY

Whatever the circumstances, Dickens, from Trinity College, Cambridge, became Master and served until his death in 1703. He was buried on 2nd March at St. Mary's, Stockport.

The early eighteenth century was the most successful period of the School's activity since its foundation. Much of this was due to the new Master, Joseph Dale, appointed by the Company without competition in Stockport on 1st December 1703. He was the son of a minister in Denton and had attended Trinity College, Oxford. His reputation became such that the School began to attract the attention of those who could well have afforded to send their children to boarding schools. Pupils came from Derbyshire and Lancashire, well beyond its traditional area. Like his predecessors Dale was a clergyman, although his remarkable success was made possible at least in part by his fortunate enjoyment of an independent income.[1]

For much of his Mastership the stipend paid by the Company actually fell below the far from lavish £10 to only £9. It was by this time not quite clear exactly which lands in the Company's possession related to the original bequest. The whole of the property had been destroyed in the Great Fire of London in 1666, and the land occupied by the three houses in Foster Lane was either soon after or by the early nineteenth century incorporated in the Goldsmiths' Hall. In the 'Old Rental' of 1682 certain properties were described as 'Proper lands' and were 'supposed' to be the benefaction of Sir Edmond; according to the Goldsmiths' records they were yielding only £56 13 4d a year between 1671 and 1720, or only a little more than half as much again as the rent receivable two centuries earlier. During Dale's tenure (1703–1752) the rents more than doubled but, of course, the Company was bound to pay only the due £10 irrespective of the actual yield, low or high, of the properties.

The early years of the eighteenth century are illustrated by events in London and Stockport. In 1712 the Goldsmiths, finding themselves responsible for yearly payments not only to the charities which they supported or were still required to pay for but also to the many hundreds of the Company's annuities over the years 1695–1709, resolved to mortgage their properties. In Stockport, the School had already benefited from the generosity of many individual local donors. The community – represented by the Mayor and Corporation of the Borough – began to organize its activity in support of the School along better defined lines. Already the local people were disposed to make over various small sums for the use of the Schoolmaster. It was the custom for the Mayor and Aldermen to receive this money on his behalf and to pay him the amount annually. On 1st August 1705 the system was changed, so that the interest on these sums should be received by the overseers of the poor and a fixed amount of £7 10 0d be paid annually to the Master. This arrangement appears to have lasted for around a century. Furthermore, in February 1711, as part of a general move to increase revenue, it was decided to sell the 'Commons and Waste Grounds' of Stockport, sufficient to yield about £60 a year; of this, one sixth was to be paid to the Mayor towards defrayment of the costs of his office, and another sixth to the Schoolmaster, while the remaining two thirds were devoted to the poor of the town. Between 1712 and 1716 the lots were sold to about twenty different persons: the same rents remained in force for the next century. The Master's share was £11 11 8d.

From 1717 Dale was also Curate of Chorlton Chapel (£10 a year) and of Birch Chapel (£3 10 0d); in 1723 he added the Chapelry of Denton (£20); and in 1733 he became Curate of St. Mary's Church in Stockport (£40 a year). While holding this post he arranged the building of a scholars' gallery at the Church, from which later Masters derived a small income. He was Rector of Taxal for a short while in 1726–27.

Between 1717 and 1734 Dale sent nineteen of his pupils to St. John's College, Cambridge, and two others to Trinity. Strangely, outside these dates, no other of his pupils has been traced: Oxford University and the other Cambridge Colleges did not then list the schools of their entrants.

Dale resigned on 20th December 1750, being almost 70 years of age. In his letter to the Goldsmiths, he offered to

'endeavour to find out a person both to answer to their expectation and those of the Town, and . . . to superintend and assist him for a while.'

The Company was pleased to accept, but things did not progress as smoothly as had been anticipated. Lady Betty Warren, the mother of the Lord of the Manor, had somehow gained the impression that her son, who appointed the Rector, Mayor, and Aldermen, had also the right to appoint the Schoolmaster. The Goldsmiths referred her to Sir Edmond's will, and she withdrew. The election of a successor eventually took place in February 1752, when two candidates presented themselves, the Rev. William Jackson and the Rev. John Chorley

Knowles. Knowles, who was then Curate of St. Mary's in Stockport, had the support of the Rector, Mayor, and Aldermen of the Town, but Jackson was recommended by nineteen other clergymen, 'other gentlemen who have had university education . . . among whom is Mr. Brooke to whom both candidates were scholars [at Manchester Grammar School]', and the Dean and Senior Fellow of Brasenose College, Oxford (whence Knowles also had graduated). In spite (or perhaps, more likely, because) of the local support for Knowles, Jackson was appointed to the post.

He had already become Curate of Denton in 1751, following on Dale's resignation of that post. He became Curate also of Newton Heath in 1789, and the Earl of Hardwick's chaplain the following year. Only one of his pupils is known, R. F. Cheetham, who praised his Master thus:

'Think you that Nature cannot climb
Above the world to such a height sublime?
Banish the thought – the tearful Muse has known
The man in whom such lofty virtue shone,
Whose heart was purely of celestial frame
And need she mention Jackson's honoured name.'

Jackson died in August 1791 and was buried in Manchester.

St. Mary's Parish Church in 1810. Only the Decorated (early 14th century) chancel survived the rebuilding to Lewis Wyatt's design in 1813–1817. Removed from the Church, the Shaa tombstone, recognizable from its coat-of-arms, survived for many years in the wall of an outhouse at 1, Northcote Street, Waterloo, Stockport, but was finally destroyed in 1902. [Reproduced by permission of the Metropolitan Borough of Stockport.]

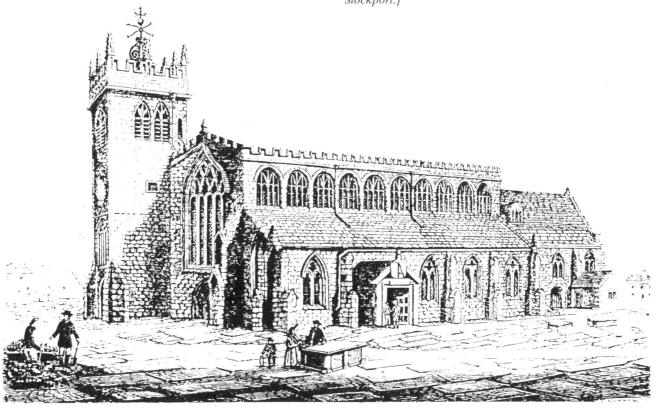

HOYLE[1]

The advertisement for a replacement was placed 'in a Cheshire paper, also in an Oxford and a Cambridge paper and in all the London papers'. Among the six candidates on the short list were the Rev. Elkanah Hoyle and the Rev. George Porter, and it was the latter, a graduate of Christ's College, Cambridge, who was appointed on 20th January 1792. In August, however, he wrote to the Goldsmiths:

'Gentlemen,

'When you did me the honour of appointing me to the Mastership of Stockport School I was led to suppose that the Income, inclusive of Ten Pounds paid by your Worshipful Company, amounted to nearly Three Hundred Pounds per annum, and from an Enquiry, however, during my Residence here, I have had the Mortification to find that the whole Salary was not more than £25 10 10½d, so that it was impossible for me to remain in the Situation without a Prospect of Church Preferment in the Neighbourhood, which I have no reason to hope for. I must beg therefore to give up the appointment and request you to accept my Resignation. Yet I cannot relinquish the Situation without expressing my Obligation for your appointment though the Emolument fell short of what I was taught to expect.

'I have the Honour to be, Gentlemen,
'With great respect, your obliged and
'very humble Servant,
'George Porter.'

In December 1792 the Goldsmiths met again to appoint a new Master, Hoyle, a graduate of Pembroke College, Cambridge, re-applied, and this time was successful. In a letter written the following April, he notes that he too 'found the endowment very small, but the Inhabitants liberal in their patronage and support'. There were various ways for the Master to supplement his income, as has been seen. Hoyle was appointed to Norbury Chapel and Poynton Chapel in March 1795, and as Chaplain to the Poynton, Worth, Norbury and Bullock Smithy Volunteers in 1803. In addition, he received three guineas a year for selling the seating rights of seven of the fourteen Grammar School pews in the Parish Church, a practice started in 1781 by Jackson for £1 10 6d. But Hoyle's greatest 'innovations' were to admit girls and to start charging fees, in direct contravention of the will. By these means, his income grew to about £300 a year. The introduction of girls was quite a novelty, as with very few exceptions the ancient grammar school foundations were generally only for boys. Sir Edmond's will had specified, however, only that the Master should teach 'all-man persons children'. Charging fees, on the other hand, was quite inadmissible: the Master should teach 'frely without any wagis or salarye asking or taking of any person, except only my salarye'.

The School buildings were by now almost 200 years old, and it is perhaps strange that there is only one contemporary description of them as a school; ' . . . there is a neat free grammar school' (*The Itinerant*, 1st May 1794). There was a much fuller description in the *Stockport Advertiser* in April 1887:

'The School was built of brick; it was a substantial building, but had no pretensions to architectural beauty. It was oblong in form about 36 feet in length and about 16 feet in width, and two storeys high. There were two windows to each room looking on Chestergate, and four windows to each room on the east side of the building. There had been windows on the westerly side of the school, but they appeared to have been built up a long time, judging from the appearance of the workmanship on the outside. It is very probable that these windows were built up when the Old School was converted into the Stockport Assembly Rooms. The Grammar School extended from the footpath in Chestergate to the brink of the Tin Brook. On the east side was a small playground, surrounded by a low brick wall. The entrance to the school was from the schoolyard, at the north side of the same.

'There were two rooms belonging to the Old Grammar School. . . . We entered the upper room by a flight of stairs leading from the north side of the yard. On the west side of the hall was a fireplace, surmounted by an antique-looking mantelpiece.'

Inside there were 'nice raised oak seatings and desks on the east and south sides, and a large imposing headmaster's desk or rostrum, with back and canopy reaching to the ceiling'.

In January 1795 Hoyle wrote to the Goldsmiths to say that the windows in the Schoolhouse needed repairing, and that the cost was estimated to be £16. He mentioned also that 'The inhabitants of the town have been so good as to rebuild me the Court wall and make some improvements in the yard, and they are very desirous for the Company to lend their aid'. Whether the Company did help is not known, and for over thirty years Hoyle went on in his own way.

We are fortunate to have exact details of the

type of education offered during this period, for in December 1817 James Moorhouse, a 13-year-old pupil at the School, wrote this letter to his Grandfather:

'My teachers desire me to address this letter to you relative to my education, that you may form some idea what progress I have made in different studies since last Midsummer. The system is regularly conducted in the following manner: Every Monday morning I either recite a piece of prose or poetry from Enfield's *Speaker*, or present a letter. During the other mornings in the week I shew English exercises and repeat English Grammar with fourteen words of spelling and the meaning of each word. Then accompts engage my attention until 11 o'clock, at which time writing commences and ends at 12. Every Tuesday and Thursday afternoons I repeat Goldsmith's *Geography* and afterwards trace on maps, Countries, Islands, Seas, and Rivers.

'I read in Goldsmith's *History of Greece*, which is a very interesting book, then my attention is directed to Arithmetic which generally finishes the day's employment. Of my writing you will form a more correct idea when you see my specimen of Penmanship, which I hope will afford you much pleasure, for my endeavours have not been deficient to render it deserving of your esteem. Dear Grandfather, I am very much indebted to you for sending me to school, and especially to my present Teachers, who have greatly contributed to my improvement, but to you is due all the knowledge I possess.

'I am
    Dear Grandfather,
      'Your Affectionate and Dutiful Grandson,
      'James Moorhouse.'

Early in 1826 Hoyle wrote again to the Goldsmiths about the School,
'setting forth the scantinesss of its yearly funds and alluding to various repairs and expenses which have been occasionally borne at his charges, amounting to about £130, and . . . the Wardens are satisfied that a very considerable increase has taken place in the Rents of the estates left for the Endowment of the School, affording means to the Company for extending the benefits of the institution'.

For the Goldsmiths and for the country the opening years of the nineteenth century were ones of financial crisis at home and of war abroad. The Company's fortunes had however recovered from their potentially disastrous state of the previous century, and the Goldsmiths had responded handsomely to many requests made of them: in 1803 they donated £1,000 to 'the patriotic fund at Lloyds

Hoyle's most distinguished pupil was George Back, born at Holly Vale House in Stockport on 6th November 1796. Having joined the Royal Navy as a midshipman, he was captured by the French in 1809, and spent the next five years as a prisoner of war. During his captivity he studied French, mathematics, and drawing. Having returned to England, he served on Franklin's expedition in search of the North-West Passage in 1817, and on two further of his voyages of exploration in North American waters in 1819 and 1823. He was promoted Lieutenant in 1823 (the cause of a celebratory banquet at the Warren Bulkeley Hotel) and Commander in 1827. In 1832 he offered to mount an expedition to search for Sir John Ross, who had sailed three years previously in search of the North-West Passage and was presumed dead. Back set sail in February 1833, and during the course of the two-year journey travelled more than 7,500 miles in Polar regions, sailing more than 400 miles along what he named the Great Fish River (now the Back River). Ross in fact returned safely while the expedition was away, and when Back himself came home King William IV appointed him Post-Captain (a rank held otherwise only by the King). Back's last voyage of discovery was in 1836–37, when in command of HMS Terror he surveyed the Polar coast from Regent's Inlet to Cape Turnagain. On all these journeys Back and his men endured terrible hardships and great dangers – temperatures as low as −50° Fahrenheit; makeshift 'meals' of leather trousers, a gun-cover, and old shoes; and attacks by Eskimos. HMS Terror was sailed home in 1837 bound together with chains and cables. Further honours and promotions came, and he died as Admiral Sir George Back, F.R.S., D.C.L., on 23rd June 1878, and was buried in Kensal Green Cemetery.
[From a drawing made in 1833 by William Brockedon; reproduced by permission of the National Portrait Gallery.]

for the relief and reward of the defenders of their Country at this Important Crisis', and in 1807 they provided £200 for a school in Londonderry, even though the Irish Society had already subscribed. But it cannot be denied that they had neglected their fixed charities. A petition to them might bring assistance for a particular project, but their schools received little attention: salaries were simply noted in the accounts and no one stopped to consider whether £10 which had been generous by the standards of earlier centuries might now be inadequate.

From this period began the Goldsmiths' new era of charitable work, which would see re-foundation and re-building, new foundations, and huge expenditure on education. A Royal Commission was established to inquire into Charities, and its chapter on the Goldsmiths' Company was published in 1822. The report was useful in pointing out the confused state of the Company's knowledge of its charities, and certainly the generosity would have been impossible without rigorous financial control (from 1810 to 1816, for example, expenditure had exceeded income by £10,000, largely because of the work on the Company's almhouses at Acton). But credit should be given where it is due, and it is clear that in the years before the report the Goldsmiths were considering – still in a vague way and mindful of the possibility of a Government Inquiry – how 'a more liberal observance of the apparent intentions of the Founders' might be effected.

The immediate impetus came from Cromer, the inhabitants of which pointed out that Sir Bartholomew Read's sixteenth-century £10 was sufficient for only ten boys, and that a new school for eighty or a hundred might be built for £250. The Goldsmiths deliberated, and in due course authorized the expenditure. Cromer had a strange relationship with the Company. It was close enough to London, and even closer to some of the Company in person. As a seaside resort it was always likely to develop, but never did. It does, however, have some significance for the history of Stockport Grammar School, for there is a sketch of the Cromer School by Philip Hardwick, the young architect who was to give Stockport's School its finest home in four centuries.

Hoyle's letter from Stockport in 1826 stirred the Company into further activity, and a visit to the School by Prime Warden Garrett, accompanied by Wardens Rundell and Hanes, confirmed their newly-awakened interest. On 19th October 1826 the Company received its first ever full Report on the School.[2]

Having returned to London, the Goldsmiths considered the subject and it is remarkable that,

Rev. E. Hoyle, M.A., Headmaster 1792–1829.

Rev. C. K. Prescot, M.A., Rector of Stockport 1820–1875.

32

after so many years in which scarcely a mention is made of Stockport in the Minute Books, it now occupied so much of their attention for five years. On 12th April 1827 they met to discuss the possibility of transferring the School to new buildings on a new site. Wellington Road had recently been constructed – a large road through open countryside to the west of the old town centre – and a new turnpike road to Cheadle was taking shape. The site in mind was where the turnpike (now called Greek Street) left Wellington Road, and was owned by the Hon. Frances Maria Warren, Lady Vernon, the Lady of the Manor. Plans were prepared, and accepted in principle at a further meeting on 1st August. The Company however was not willing simply to spend money, but intended to have somewhat closer control than had been the case in the more recent past.[3]

After the School removed to Greek Street, the Chestergate premises had many uses: Assembly and Exhibition Rooms; a school again, run by Mr. Edward Nuttall from 1837 to 1840; a Mission Hall; a shop; a warping room; a draper's shop; until they were burnt down in 1882. A plaque now marks the site.

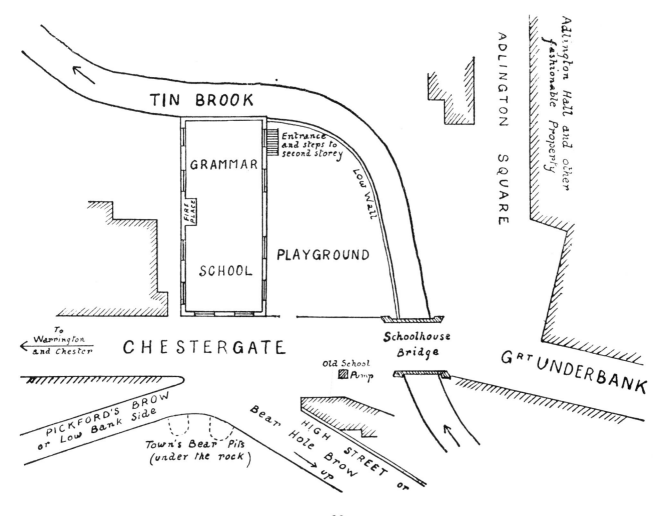

Buildings were quickly erected along the 'New Road', one of the earliest being the National School, shown here, on the site of the present Town Hall. The Foundation Stone was laid in 1825, and the building opened the next year. There was one full-time master, whose salary was £65. A Sunday School at first, it operated also as a day school from 1831, with 1,253 pupils on the register at its peak. Boys used the lower classroom, 104 feet long by 40 wide and 15 high, girls the upper (104 by 40 by 26). The population of Stockport increased from 14,830 in the 1801 census to over 53,000 by 1871. In 1833 the Report of the Factory Commission listed 50 public and private schools in the town with 1,899 pupils, as well as 14 Sunday schools with 5,243 pupils. By 1879 Board Schools alone had more than 10,000 pupils on the registers.

As well as giving the land for the Grammar School at the corner of Greek Street (probably so-named because that subject was taught at the School), in 1843 Lady Vernon also gave the land for the British School opposite and for St. Thomas's School nearby on Hillgate.

[Reproduced by permission of the Metropolitan Borough of Stockport.]

Stockport in 1824, as surveyed for Baines's 'Gazetteer'. The 'New Road' is Wellington Road South, and a Toll Bar stands on the turnpike to Cheadle, the as yet un-named Greek Street. In the town centre, no. 11 on Chestergate marks the then site of the School. The School's probable first home is St. Mary's Parish Church, no. 1.

The expansion of the town had begun with silk-throwing (introduced from Derby in the 18th century) which was quickly followed by cotton-spinning and weaving, using the abundant supplies of fast-flowing water in the vicinity – the Tin or Carr Brook, and the Rivers Tame, Goyt, and Mersey. Industry attracted people from the countryside, and the population continued to grow – 25,469 by 1831, 53,001 by 1871. Cotton became king in the North West, with over 40 mills in Stockport alone: but times were often hard – because of overproduction in the 1840s, for instance, at one stage there were 51% out of work and 31% on short time; and the disruption to the cotton trade during the American Civil War was also severe.

[Reproduced by permission of the Metropolitan Borough of Stockport.]

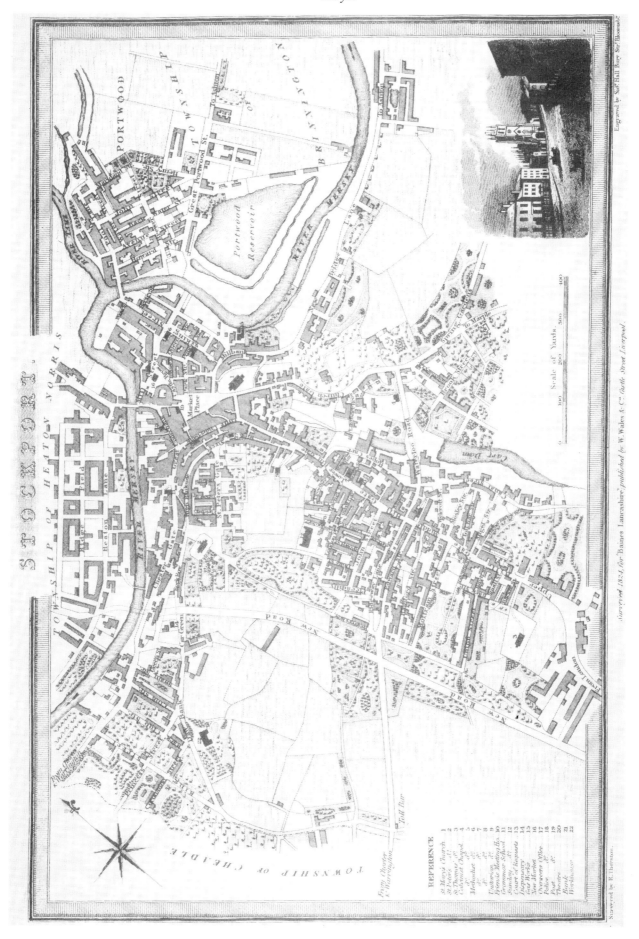

GREEK STREET

In 1829 events moved quickly. Philip Hardwick, the Goldsmiths' surveyor, was appointed architect on 18th February; on 18th March Hoyle's death was reported to London, and duly regretted; on 27th March the transfer of property was ordered to be carried out forthwith, and the Rev. William Newstead, then Usher and in charge of the School since Hoyle's death, was allowed to continue in office. On 8th September the Chestergate site was sold to Mr. J. K. Winterbottom, Lady Vernon's Agent, and the new site acquired. On 1st October the Goldsmiths met to consider – and to reject – proposals sent from Stockport for the new School. Closer supervision of the day-to-day running was still their aim. While the system of instruction was pondered upon further, Hardwick's work continued apace. During March 1830 his drawings for the new building were approved, and tenders were invited for the work, which comprised both a school for 150 pupils and a house for the Headmaster. Various quotations were considered by the Goldsmiths on 1st July, and the contract was awarded to the Warrington company of Hinde and Haddock, at an estimated cost of £3,526.[1]

The Foundation Stone of the new building was laid on Wednesday, 8th September, 1830. The Prime Warden, together with Mr. Warden Blanchard, the Surveyor, and the Clerk, journeyed from London to perform the ceremony. These were joined at the site by the Stockport contingent – a large assembly of local dignitaries, together with the builders and two bands. When the Prime Warden had laid the stone and tested it for square and level, the Rector of Stockport offered prayers for success, and the ceremony concluded with cheers for the Goldsmiths and their munificence.

Hardwick visited Stockport regularly while the work was in progress, allowing the Clerk to pay the builders in instalments: £600 on 11th November, £400 on 13th January, 1831, £600 on 24th March, £800 on 30th June. By 6th October he was able to report that only some papering and painting remained to be done; by the 20th he could recommend payment of the final instalment.

The Foundation Stone of the new School at Greek Street was hollowed out to contain contemporary mementoes: an engraved brass tablet and a glass jar (holding a sovereign, a half-sovereign, a crown, a half-crown, a shilling, a sixpence, a penny, a halfpenny, and a farthing).

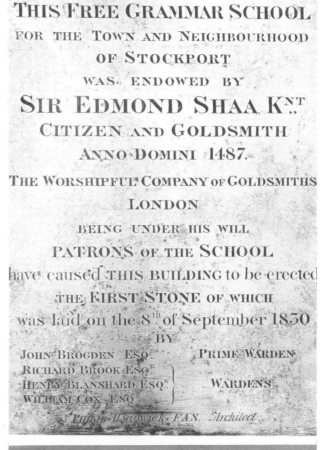

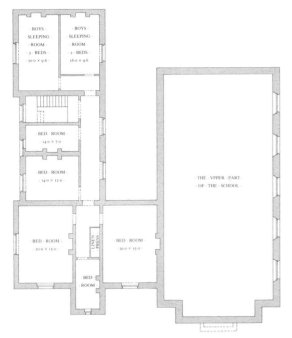

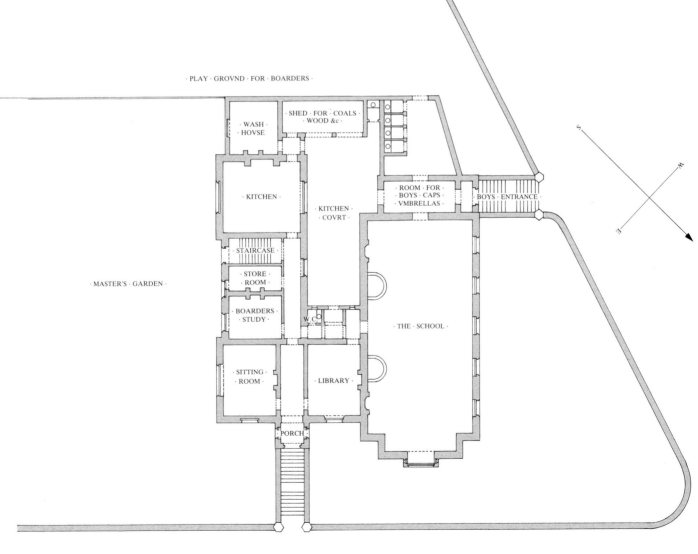

Hardwick's 1829 plans for the new School at Greek Street. Above – the first floor; below – at ground level. The schoolroom was 60 feet long by 30 wide, occupying the whole height of the building. The roof timbers were exposed to view, the beams resting on corbels.
[Reproduced by permission of the Worshipful Company of Goldsmiths][2]

Hardwick's drawing of the Schoolroom from Greek Street. At the right is the boys' entrance.
[Reproduced by permission of the Worshipful Company of Goldsmiths.]

Hardwick's sections through the Schoolroom show several of the internal arrangements – for fireplaces, doors, and desks, as well as for roof and foundations.
[Reproduced by permission of the Worshipful Company of Goldsmiths.]

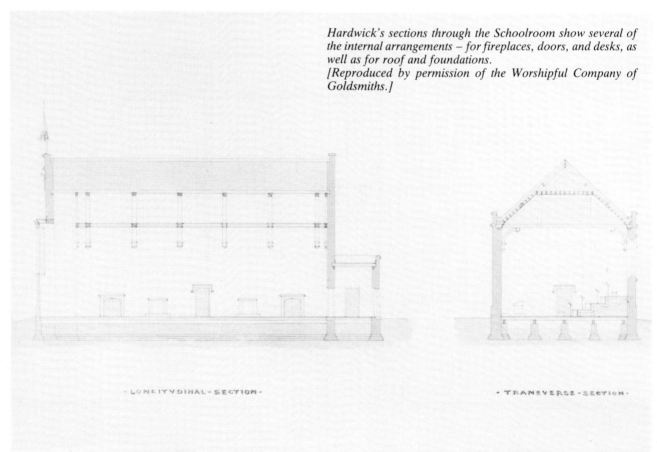

· LONGITUDINAL · SECTION ·   · TRANSVERSE · SECTION ·

Hardwick's drawings of the east and south fronts. The east front faced Wellington Road South. To the right is the Schoolroom; above the window is a massive representation of the arms of the Goldsmiths' Company (now to be found in the driveway below the Hall at Buxton Road). Sir Edmond Shaa's coat of arms shown below the window was in fact inserted above the doorway; below the window was the Foundation Stone instead. The south front, with its recessed centre and projecting gables, looked onto the Headmaster's Garden.
[Reproduced by permission of the Worshipful Company of Goldsmiths.]

- EAST-FRONT -

- SOUTH-FRONT -

39

MIDDLETON

There now arose the question of the appointment of a new Headmaster: Newstead, appointed Usher in 1826 and temporary Headmaster since Hoyle's death in 1829, was also Assistant Curate at St. Peter's Church, and was a minister first and schoolmaster second. From St. Peter's he went to Selby in 1836, but stayed there only a year before returning as incumbent of Chadkirk Chapel in Romiley, where he served until his death in 1862.

The post of Headmaster was widely advertised, and the attraction of new buildings produced thirteen applicants, drawn from all over the country. The Goldsmiths reverted to their former practice, abandoned for a century, of requiring the personal appearance in London of all the candidates, from amongst whom the Rev. Thomas Middleton, 29 years of age and an Oxford graduate, was chosen. The new man was soon in contact with Hardwick, who travelled to Stockport to discuss fittings for the School and who presented on 26th July what he probably thought was to be his final report,

'shewing the total expenditure in the erection of the Free Grammar School at Stockport amounting to £4,499 15 7d, of which £3,488 6 0d had been paid, leaving a balance of £1,011 9 7d still due to some of the tradesmen employed.'

'He also laid before the Meeting an account of the expenses he had incurred in travelling &c during the progress of the building, as also his charge of Commission, together amounting to £388 13 8d of which he had received on account £100, Whereupon the Committee were pleased to order the balance to be paid him.'

Hardwick's involvement might have ended there, if it had not been for one of the tradesmen, who addressed a petition to the Company nine months later: his original estimate of £2,514 18 1¼d had left him bearing a loss of £266 6 3¾d. He explained his problem and, to support his case, produced the opinion of another builder:

'that from the style of the building (which although ancient in its design, is at the present day unique and novel) it is almost impossible to calculate to any thing near the real cost, where the greatest part of the expense is incurred by the labour in working the stone in the various forms on antique architecture.'

Hardwick recommended that the man's loss should be paid, even though there could be no legal claim, and this was done. He was a skilled architect who would grow used to praise, but he must have been pleased to hear that the Goldsmiths regarded his school as 'not excelled by any other building of a similar construction in solidity, taste, and execution.'

The new building, in the style of Tudor Gothic, was opened for public inspection on 23rd April 1832 and opened formally, with even greater ceremony than when the foundation stone had been laid, exactly a week later. The procession that attended this time was impressive:

The Beadle
The Javelinmen
Band of Music
Apparitors of St. Mary's, St. Peter's, and St. Thomas's Churches
110 scholars, three abreast
The Usher of the School
Assistant Constables
Deputy Constables
Constables
Churchwardens
Aldermen, two abreast
Bailiff of the Manor
Mayor and Steward
The Magistrates

The Rev. C. K. Prescot (Rector) and Clergy
The Rev. Thomas Middleton, Master
The Prime Warden and Wardens of the Goldsmiths' Company, Governors and Patrons of the School, with their Solicitor and Architect
120 Gentlemen of the neighbourhood, four abreast

Speeches were made, the Goldsmiths were thanked, prayers were offered, and the building was declared open.

As well as paying for the new building, the Goldsmiths also increased the salaries of the Headmaster and Usher, made the School free again to the scholars, and paid the running costs. The Headmaster's salary was now £200, plus the £10 from Sir Edmond's endowment, together with the use of a house, free from rent and taxes. He could supplement his income by taking up to eight boarders, but he was forbidden to accept any curacy or other parochial duty without the Goldsmiths' consent. While the new salary was a vast improvement on what it had been, it must be remembered that the salary of the High Master at Manchester Grammar School at the time was £420, together with house.

Middleton had to submit monthly reports to the Company, with full reports at Midsummer and

Christmas, and the Goldsmiths themselves proposed to visit the School annually in June to conduct a Public Examination. While the Headmaster taught the Latin and Greek, the Usher, appointed by the Governors at a salary of £105, attended to the 'three Rs' and English Grammar. (His counterpart in Manchester received £220, together with a house).

The first Usher to be appointed was Mr. William Bayles, of Barnard Castle in Co. Durham, 'a very successful teacher, especially in Grammar and Arithmetic, but impatient when overwrought.' He and the Headmaster were the sole teachers of some 150 pupils for a school day which lasted from 8am until noon and 2 till 5pm (4pm from November until March). There were holidays of one month in the Summer and at Christmas, with shorter breaks at Easter and Whitsun, and Wednesday and Saturday were half-holidays. Entrants to the School were to be no younger than six nor older than ten, nor could they stay without special consent beyond the age of fourteen. The better pupils then went off to a boarding school. King William's College on the Isle of Man was a favourite.

To assist in the local management of the School, the Goldsmiths appointed a Committee of Visitors, of which both the Mayor and the Rector were ex-officio members. The first Mayor so to be honoured was, appropriately enough, Mr. Winterbottom, Lady Vernon's Steward, who was Mayor in 1831 and 1832. Other members of the first Committee were the Lord Bishop of Chester, Lord Vernon, the Rev. H. Raikes (Chancellor of the Diocese), John Isherwood of Marple Hall, Captain Sir Salusbury Pryce Humphreys of Bramall Hall, Joseph Bruckshaw of Harrytown Hall, and William Dysart of Mile End Hall.

The body now known as the Worshipful Company of Goldsmiths of London received its first Royal Charter on 13th March 1327, but its organization as a group of craftsmen dates back to at least the 12th Century. It was the first guild to have its own headquarters, for in June 1339 nineteen goldsmiths bought a house in Foster Lane. The present Hall, shown here, on the same site in London, was under construction at the same time as the Greek Street School, and was designed by the same architect, Hardwick. Covering about half an acre and magnificently Palladian in style, it cost £106,190 17 9d, and was opened in 1835.
[Reproduced by permission of the Worshipful Company of Goldsmiths.]

The first of the Annual Reports under the new regime is perhaps of special interest and deserves quoting at some length:

'. . . we attended at the School on Monday the 17th [July, 1833] and found that it was divided into six classes, the first being composed of three boys only whose study was the Classics, the second of about 20 who were instructed in the Latin Grammar, and the remaining four classes were composed of boys whose education was confined to Reading, Writing, Arithmetic, and English Grammar, in which instruction the boys in the two senior classes also participated.'

'We then proceeded with the examination of the boys in the presence of the Mayor and several Ladies and Gentlemen of the Town, Mr. Prescott [sic] the Rector of Stockport being the Examiner; and considering the recent re-endowment and establishment of the School, and that many of the children when first admitted were unable to read, and the majority very backward in their learning, we have much pleasure in reporting that the result of this first public examination was very satisfactory and that it was apparent that the Master and Usher had faithfully discharged their duties.'

'The examination being closed we then distributed under the recommendation of the Examiner various Books to the boys who had chiefly distinguished themselves as a reward for assiduity and good conduct, and as an incitement to future exertions which were received by them with marked satisfaction.'

'The following morning the Deputation again visited the School previous to the Scholars being dismissed for the Midsummer Holidays, and having inspected the Book of Entry of the Scholars' Admissions &c we found that the whole number of 150 had been received into the School – that on the day of examination 141 were present and the remaining 9 absent from suspension or illness and one by death.'

The mention of suspension is of interest: that the cause of it – truancy – is not only a 20th century phenomenon is shown by the next paragraph of the Report:

'The parent of George Highton who had been suspended on account of frequent absence attended by order of the Deputation and stated that he had 3 boys in the School and that the one complained of was so refractory as to be beyond his management and would not attend as he should, frequently persuading his Brothers to follow his example and having gone into service he wished him to be dismissed, which was done, and the parent was informed that if the other two were not more regular in their attendance they would also be discharged.'

The Report ends on a higher note:

'We cannot close the report without mentioning the great satisfaction expressed by the Mayor and Corporation and Inhabitants of the Town of Stockport at the re-establishment of the School, and the high sense they entertained of the liberality and kindness of the Goldsmiths' Company.'

'J. B. Smith, W. Bateman (Wardens), Jas Tomlin, James Henderson, Saml Haynes.

'Goldsmiths' Hall, 25th June, 1833.'

The Goldsmiths themselves were pleased with their creation, and showed their satisfaction in practical ways.[1] More land was purchased for playgrounds in 1837 and 1839; a rent-free house for the Usher was added in 1839. For those pupils wishing to proceed to University, two Exhibitions of £50 each were instituted in 1837. Middleton sought, and obtained, the Company's consent to his becoming an Evening Lecturer at St. Thomas's Church in Stockport, a Morning Lecturer at St. Michael's Church in Manchester, and a Surrogate for Stockport and District. He was even granted £10 to enable him to keep his garden in order, though the Goldsmiths proved obdurate to his continual requests for a Stable and Chaisehouse. The Usher's salary was increased from £105 to 150 guineas.

Pride in the new School was also shown by the boys, who raised £15 for a new banner in blue silk. On one side were the Goldsmiths' Company's arms, in gold, four yards in diameter, with the legend 'Free Grammar School, Stockport'; on the other the arms again, with 'Founded and Endowed by Sir Edmond Shaa, Knight, 1487; Re-endowed by the Worshipful the Goldsmiths' Company, 1832' in gold letters. This new banner complemented the old, in white silk, with 'Ancient Grammar School, Vivat Rex' on one side, and

'ingenuas didicisse fideliter artes
emollit mores, nec sinit esse feros'

on the other. The quotation is from the Roman poet Ovid (*Epistulae ex Ponto, 2.9.47/8*) and may be rendered 'to have studied faithfully the liberal arts refines the character and forbids it to be uncouth'.

Sir Edmond's other foundation, the little Chapel at Woodhead, had not been so fortunate: in May 1837 the Goldsmiths received

'Applications . . . from the principal House holders of the Chapelry of Woodhead in the Parish of Mottram in Longdendale in the County of Chester . . . praying assistance in support of their institutions.'

The building was in great need of repair but the Company, unaware for centuries of its existence, felt unable to contribute.

The 1830s and early 1840s were successful years at the School. The 1837 Visitation, for instance, reported

'that the highest praise they can bestow on the Masters is merited by them. Such indeed are the attainments of some of the Scholars that at no distant period some further assistance will be required by the Masters – and also an increased allowance for the purchase of books.'

By 1842 it had indeed proved necessary to expand the staff, and Mr. Sharpe, a master from the National Schools in London, was appointed to assist Bayles. Middleton was granted £100 to enable him to furnish his house. It also became commonplace for boys to request, and be granted, extensions to their stay in the School, and the Exhibitions to Oxford and Cambridge on offer from the Company were regularly taken up. The 1844 Report hints however that there had been some decline in standards at the lower end of the School, and urged that 'prior to admission the Boys should be able to read and write and have learned the first principles of English grammar. It also suggested that the age range should be from 8 years to 16 (instead of 6 to 14), and in 1848 the lower age was in fact raised to 7.

In 1845 the 'Railway Mania' began, when the plans for new lines submitted to Parliament would, if passed and carried out, have more than trebled the country's railway mileage. It appears that Middleton was a victim. The Goldsmiths heard by means of anonymous reports that he was often absent, attending meetings of the Manchester and Birmingham Railway Co. during school hours, and also that he had become Rector of Northenden. His absences seem to have influenced Bayles, who was likewise alleged to be often away, his duties being performed by monitors. It was also said that both masters neglected to wear their gowns, that the gardens were overgrown, and that, though there were still about 150 boys at the School, yet 'they were of a lower class than formerly'. The number of Visitors had dwindled to three – the Rector (the Rev. C. K. Prescot), Mr. P. E.

Marsland (the Mayor), and Mr. J. Marsland (the last two being Old Boys of the School).

Middleton and Bayles attempted to defend themselves against the allegations, but the 1846 Report mentions the Examiners' surprise at 'the gross ignorance of the boys in divinity'. The conclusion was that 'the School has fallen off lamentably in the higher branches of education'. The Goldsmiths accepted with alacrity Middleton's offer to resign owing to 'daily declining health' on 27th April 1847, but were unwilling to honour his final request:

'Having given you the best years of my life, I now appeal to your justice and well-known liberality for a retiring pension, humbly requesting that in the event of my death the same may be continued to my child for his education till he attains 15 years of age, he being now in his 7th year.'

Middleton's fears for his health were unfounded. He stayed as Rector at Northenden until 1849, and then moved to St. George's in Manchester, where he remained until he died in 1875 – 28 years later!

Hardwick's best-known building was perhaps the Doric portico (often, but wrongly, called 'Arch'), built as an entrance to the Euston Station of the London and Birmingham Railway Co. in May 1837. Behind it was Hardwick's Great Hall, dating from 1846. Both Portico and Hall were demolished in the 1960s during the rebuilding of the station, despite strenuous efforts to save them.
[Reproduced by permission of Millbrook House Ltd.]

GURNEY

Following upon Middleton's resignation and the other revelations, the Goldsmiths decided that the School required a new Headmaster, new Visitors, and new Statutes. The first was obviously the most pressing, and on 29th July 1847 Mr. William Gurney, aged only 25 and a Cambridge graduate, was appointed. Among the new Visitors was Mr. Richard Sykes, of Edgeley, beginning a family tradition of service to the School which was to last over a century. New Statutes were not finally approved until November of the following year, after much discussion.

In May 1847 a Deputation travelled from Stockport to London to request the addition of French, German, and the higher classes of Mathematics: 'the most respectable branches of the inhabitants of the Town would willingly contribute towards the additional expenses this enlarged system of Education would create.' Other pieces of 'advice' accompanied this:

'Your Memorialists would be glad if the School could be placed in such a position as to enable them to send their children to it with a reasonable expectation that their manners would not be corrupted by the admission of a class of boys more fitted for National Schools than Grammar Schools. There are sufficient inhabitants in Stockport for a good Grammar School, but without a department for the teaching the modern languages the school can be of comparatively little use in a commercial population like that of Stockport. We your Memorialists therefore pray that your Worshipful Company will reduce the number of scholars to such an amount as will ensure scholars with whom a tradesman's son ought to associate, leaving others to go to the National Schools.'

In the face of a petition such as this, backed by the signatures of 105 of Stockport's most eminent and respected citizens, the Goldsmiths were in an awkward position, which they decided to resolve by re-reading Sir Edmond's will, to see what the Founder himself had intended: a classical school (teaching Greek and Latin), without fees or social distinctions, but depending only on a willingness to learn. When they finally appeared the new Statutes were a reasoned compromise, but nevertheless they contained some fundamental changes. The Headmaster no longer had to be a clergyman (though Gurney in fact became a deacon in 1848 and was eventually ordained in 1853). The School

was to be divided into an Upper Section of 100 pupils and a Lower of 50. Fees of two guineas a year were to be charged in the Upper (books and stationery extra); the Lower was still free. The minimum age for admission became 7, and for leaving 16. School was to open at 9am, and the Summer holidays now extended to six weeks. Lastly, the School was now to be called 'The Stockport Grammar and Free Schools'.

The first Visitation under the new Headmaster took place between 19th and 21st June, 1848; present from Stockport were the Rev. C. K. Prescot and the Rev. J. Taylor, the Mayor, Mr. Newton, Mr. Sykes, and Mr. Marsland. 105 boys were enrolled in six classes, the numbers in each being 8, 15, 28, 20, 15, and 19. The Examination was conducted by the Rev. Mr. Hiley, a Fellow of St. John's College, Cambridge, and the School's troubles seemed to have passed. Indeed the Goldsmiths were so pleased that they granted the headmaster £20 to tidy his garden, and decided to extend the playground yet again. (Further additions were to be made in 1851 and 1853.) Within a month a master for the Lower School (Mr. C. F. Howell) had been appointed at £130 a year, and within four months the number of permitted boarders was increased from six to eight.

By the time of the 1849 Visitation, significant progress was obvious: there were now 130 pupils in nine classes, with 21 prospective applicants for places. The Report ends:

'In concluding this Report the Undersigned have the greatest pleasure in bearing testimony to the zeal and ability of Mr. Gurney, in which they are joined by the Visitors who attended the Examination. No reasonable doubt can exist that the School will attain under his supervision a much higher rank in the estimation of the Inhabitants of Stockport and that it will prove of very great importance and advantage to its community.

'[signed] J. B. Smith Prime Warden; James Garrard.'

Towards the end of 1849 Gurney wrote to the Goldsmiths to request £200 'to enable him to clear off his debts and leave some money for general purposes'; he was granted £300. The next year brought the first indications of the troubles which were eventually to lead to the Goldsmiths' abandonment of the School a decade later.

Mr. James Bayley, a Unitarian Minister from Heaviley, wrote to the Headmaster to object to the teaching of the Thiry-nine Articles of the Church of England. His letter evoked the surprising reply that the Headmaster could not alter the Bible, and when Bayley wrote again to point out, reasonably enough, that he could not find the Articles in his

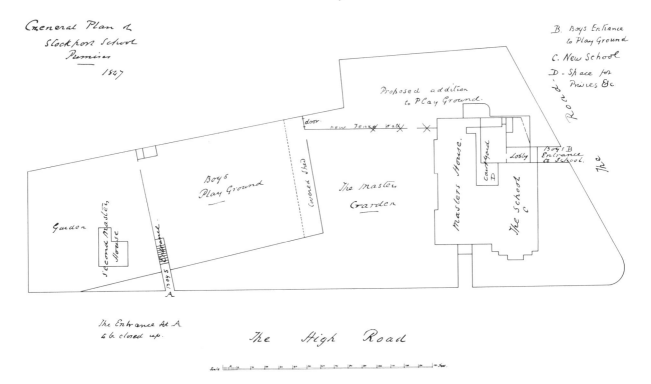

General Plan of
Stockport School
Premises
1847

B. Boys Entrance
to Play Ground

C. New School

D - Space for
Privies &c

The Road

Proposed addition
to Play Ground

new fenced Walk

door

Masters House.

Courtyard
D

Lobby

Boys B
Entrance
to School

The School
C

Boys
Play Ground

Corner Shed

The Masters
Garden

Garden

Second Master's
House

Boys

A

The Entrance At A
to be closed up.

The   High   Road

Scale

Plan of the Greek Street School in 1847, showing the extended playgrounds, gardens, and the Second Master's House. In time, the Technical College came to occupy first the playground and then the Second Master's house and Garden.
[Reproduced by permission of the Worshipful Company of Goldsmiths.]

copy of the Authorized Version, Gurney replied frostily 'I beg to decline all future disputing on the subject'. Bayley appealed to the Visitors, one of whom, Mr. Sykes, the Mayor, passed on his letter to the Goldsmiths. They informed the Headmaster in April that 'the 39 Articles are not to form any part of the tuition of the Schools and are not to be enforced'. He quickly wrote to London to apologise, and asked if he might use Dr. Watt's 'Short View of the Whole Scripture History', asserting that 'the author was a Dissenter, and the introduction of it into the School is not likely to create any fresh difficulty'. Despite the intervention of one of the Town's Members of Parliament, Mr. James Kershaw, a Dissenter himself, a Liberal, and a well-known opponent of religious endowments (which the School effectively was), the affair blew over as quickly as it had begun, for Bayley removed his sons from the School at the end of the Summer Term.[1]

There was more serious friction between the Headmaster and the Usher. After investigations by the Company, Bayles was found to have usurped the Headmaster's authority by selling stationery and interfering with book orders and he

was allowed to resign on 2nd June 1851, 'with regret, after 19 years' service'. Howell was appointed in his place, at a salary of 150 guineas. The Annual Examinations took place and evidence of continued improvement was forthcoming.

In 1852

'The Deputation have the satisfaction to state that the boys acquitted themselves exceedingly well, particularly the higher classes, some of the senior boys giving evidence of great talent and ability, especially in Mathematics.'

The usual prizes of books were presented, together with special prizes of mathematical instruments to C. E. Norris, and artists' colours to Thomas Ashe, both outstanding pupils. The Deputation also received a copy of Resolutions recently passed at a

45

Special Meeting of Visitors, but in its opinion it was

'not advisable to adopt the suggestions of the Visitors: the School in its present state works exceedingly well and it is very doubtful if a more extended course of the higher branches of education would be equally beneficial to the great mass of residents in Stockport and its vicinity, who are anxious to avail themselves of the instruction afforded to their children in the School as at present constituted.'

The success of Peter Medd, an Old Boy and son of one of the Visitors, in gaining a First Class Honours degree at Oxford so pleased the Goldsmiths that he was given a prize of £20 and the School an extra week's holiday that summer. The Headmaster was given a £50 increase in salary. He was at that time receiving £210, together with £20 for coal, £10 for cleaning, and £10 for gardening. He wrote to thank the Goldsmiths, but also had the temerity to ask 'if they considered him bound to continue in his office for some considerable time longer and not to seek a more remunerative one'. Formally but icily they replied that they 'do not desire to interfere with any views which he may have towards improving his position in life, but they expect that he will give them six months' notice of his intention to resign the mastership of the School'.[2]

The 1850s were years of continued academic success on the one hand, but on the other of simmering discontent on the part of some prominent members of the town about the School and in particular its Headmaster, into which the Goldsmiths' Company were dragged as unwilling participants. Throughout the decade the numbers in the School were maintained at almost the maximum level (100 in the Upper, Grammar School and 50 in the Lower, Free School); more land was bought by the Company for playgrounds and gardens; an extra room was added to Mr. Howell's house at a cost of £150. When he fell ill in 1857 he was granted £30 to enable him to get away for the winter, and six months' leave of absence shortly afterwards. Upon his death his widow was granted a pension of £30 a year for five years.

For all their generosity the Goldsmiths deserved thanks, and gratitude; they received nothing but complaints, and petitions. The petitions were for the introduction of French and German as main subjects; the former was admittedly already in the syllabus, but was taught on Wednesday and Saturday afternoons, not in the main timetable. The matter dragged on, year after year, until in 1857 it was decided that an extra master should be appointed, so that there could be two classes, one learning French and the other German, running at the same time for one hour, and then changing over. The lessons were timetabled on Wednesday from 12 noon until 2.10 pm, and Saturday from 10 am until 12.10 pm. The extra 10 minutes allowed was evidently for the classes (or the masters) to move. At the same time the fees were raised to £4 a year to pay for this, and Book-keeping as a subject was dropped.[3,4]

Inspired probably by the continuing ill-feeling towards himself, Gurney had attempted to leave the Grammar School by applying for the Mastership of Wellington College early in 1855, but the Goldsmiths declined to supply a testimonial of his conduct until he had given up his post, and his application therefore lapsed. Meanwhile Pope, the master of the Lower School, had been compelled to resign through ill-health at the end of 1854. He wrote to ask the Goldsmiths to appoint his brother-in-law, the Rev. Jeremiah Coombes, in his place, as otherwise he would be 'without means of support', and this they did. Pope was given a leaving present of £25, soon supplemented by a further £25 to his widow. Coombes's salary was £100, together with an additional £30 'for a residence'. His appointment was the success story of this period, and even when the Goldsmiths eventually washed their hands of the School, they continued to help him with gifts to the Church to which he had been appointed in Portwood.

Academically, the School prospered: Thomas Ashe was given a special Exhibition at St. John's College, Cambridge (the other two were already taken up), and when Howell died in August 1858 Mr. C. E. Norris, an Old Boy and a previous Goldsmiths' Exhibitioner at St. John's College, Cambridge, was appointed to take over.

A hint of the depth of feeling in Stockport appeared in the *Stockport Advertiser* on 4th June 1856, when tenders were invited for the building of a new grammar school in Shaw Heath. The instigator of this rival was the Town Clerk, Maj. Henry Coppock, Liberal and Dissenter, and his new school, the Stockport High School, eventually opened on 27th July 1857, having been built on Dodge Hill at a cost of £1,250. The Headmaster was the Rev. C. G. Hamilton, MA, and the Patron the Lord Stanley of Alderley, President of the Board of Trade. The fees were substantial for the time – ten guineas for pupils under 12, and fifteen for those older. Books and stationery were charged for in addition. The curriculum covered the Classics, English, Mathematics, French, German, Italian, and Drawing. One of the Statutes of the school is of particular interest, in view of the troubles at the Grammar School:

The east front of the Greek Street building, from Wellington Road.
[Reproduced by permission of the Worshipful Company of Goldsmiths.]

'22. The headmaster may if he think proper read each day on the opening of school such prayers as may have been previously approved of by the Governors, but no sectarian comments nor any doctrinal teaching may be allowed in the school.'

Only the Annual General Meetings of the Board in 1858 and 1859 are recorded – extremely briefly – in the Minute Books, for by 1860 the High School had ceased to exist as a separate entity. Matters regarding the Grammar School had come to a head.

Major Coppock's rival Stockport High School was planned originally to be built in Shaw Heath, but when that plan fell through it was erected on Dodge Hill. The High School lasted only three years, until 1860, but the building still survives, used today and for many years past as Christadelphian Meeting Rooms.

THE BREAK[1]

The Goldsmiths, exasperated that all their efforts should be unappreciated, had finally lost their patience. In March 1859, they commissioned a report from their Clerk on 'getting rid of the Burthen of the School'. He lost no time: his report was completed by the end of the month, and early in April they met to consider the Report and its Recommendation. The Minutes record:

'After which it was moved by Mr. James Bogle Smith seconded and unanimously resolved that the Court are of opinion that the School at Stockport should be discontinued and that the Court approves generally of the suggestions submitted to their consideration for discontinuing the School and refers the matter to the Standing Committee to open such communication with the Corporation of Stockport and the Master of the School as they may consider it desirable to make, with a view to carry the suggested plan into effect.'

When the news reached Stockport there was consternation. In spite of further petitions and letters from the town the Goldsmiths were unmoved. They had spent many thousands of pounds, first on building a fine new School, and then on equipping it and running it. The undoubted academic success was welcome and pleasing to the Goldsmiths, and they had done their best to reconcile the Headmaster and his critics. The decision to break was not taken in haste, but the culmination of years of little niggles which seemed to have no end in sight.

A deputation from Stockport travelled to London on 21st May to receive the conditions of transfer:

'1. The Governors will require that the School Buildings and premises connected therewith be kept up and in a good state of repair.

'2. That the Corporation do maintain a good and efficient School, whereof a Free School, at which not less than 30 boys are to be educated, shall form a part.

'3. That the nomination of Boys to the School shall be made fairly and without favouritism and that the Corporation shall not permit them to be influenced by political considerations, whether arising out of local or general politics.

'4. That the Schools shall be conducted as heretofore on the principles of the Church of England, but not to the exclusion of the Children of Dissenters who desire to avail themselves thereof. No Dissenters from that Church shall be appointed a Master of the School. This condition shall be accepted by the Corporation bona fide.

'5. On the foregoing conditions the Goldsmiths' Company will grant to the Corporation a lease of the School Buildings and Land connected therewith free of rent for 999 years, and will give them a perpetual endowment of £290 per annum in addition to the sum of £10 which they are bound to pay under the will of Sir Edmond Shaa; but the Lease and the Endowment Grant shall contain clauses giving the Goldsmiths' Company the right of re-entry in the one case and making the annuity to cease in the other on breach of any or either of the conditions above named.'

Several questions were put by the Deputation and answered, and then the Mayor told the Committee that the Corporation was 'very sensible of the liberality of the offer made by the Goldsmiths' Company'. He expressed the hope that a 'definitive answer would be sent from the Corporation of Stockport at an early day'.

The Town Clerk wrote the letter of acceptance on 8th June, and a Scheme of Administration drawn up by the Charity Commissioners, now involved because of the change in status of the School, was ratified at Stockport County Court on 20th January 1860. The Goldsmiths allowed Gurney £300, Norris £200, and Coombes £150 'in consideration of their services', having dismissed them the previous April with effect from 25th March 1860.

At a meeting on 26th March 1860, the Town Council met to elect its twelve trustees, now that it controlled the School. Those elected were the Mayor and seven other councillors, the magistrates' clerk, an Anglican clergyman, and a local industrialist. The Chairman was to be the Right. Rev. James Prince Lee, Lord Bishop of Manchester. This list was open to objections, and these were duly raised by Mr. Charles Baker, J.P., one of the Grammar School Visitors in the 1850s. Of the Trustees just elected, he pointed out that five were Dissenters and one (Coppock) a Unitarian. The House of Lords was deliberating at that moment whether such people could legally be Trustees of a Church of England School (it was eventually decided that they could not). Furthermore, Coppock also owned the High School, and three other of the Grammar School Trustees were Visitors of this rival. Finally, the Bishop had been appointed without being first approached.

The Charity Commissioners considered the problem, and asked the Goldsmiths for advice, the latter being well versed in the difficulties that some of Stockport's inhabitants could cause. The Company was extremely diplomatic, and hinted that it would probably be a good idea if the Rector of St. Mary's, the Vicar of St. Peter's, and Mr. John Meridyth (another Grammar School Visitor from the 1850s), who were considered to be at the root of the trouble, were not appointed Trustees.

During April and May the composition of the Board of Trustees fluctuated, as first a new Chairman (Mr. W. D. Davenport of Bramall Hall) was found, and then six new members to replace those objected to. The Company's hint was taken, and on 6th July the Charity Commissioners approved the new Board, which met for the first time twelve days later and agreed to advertise for a Headmaster who – after all the fuss and contrary to what may have been expected – was required to be an Anglican clergyman!

Gurney, probably wisely, did not apply for the post. Since leaving in March, he had set up a private school in St. Peter's Parsonage, with about sixty pupils from his old school. This lasted for two years, until he became Headmaster of Doncaster Grammar School, where he stayed until 1881. Between 1882 and 1885 he was British Chaplain in Switzerland, returning to become Vicar of Brompton Regis in Somerset. He died in 1894.

Hamilton had been appointed Acting Headmaster of the Grammar School on Gurney's departure, and had overseen the move from Dodge Hill to Greek Street of pupils, desks, and fitments, and was the successful candidate from amongst the thirteen (including one layman) who applied. He was appointed on 3rd September 1860, and signed officially on the following day:

'I Charles Gillingham Hamilton M.A. of Stockport in the Borough of Stockport and County of Chester, Clerk, a Clergyman of the Church of England, in priest's orders and a Graduate of the University of Dublin declare that I will discharge always to the best of my ability the duties of Headmaster of the Stockport Grammar and Free School, and that in case I shall be removed from my Office I will thereupon relinquish all claim to the Office and its future emoluments and I will deliver up possession of the School and my residence to the Trustees and that it shall be lawful for them in the same case without ejectment or other legal process to take possession of my residence and remove myself and my effects therefrom.'

'Dated the fourth day of September One Thousand Eight Hundred and Sixty.'

'[Signed] Charles Gillingham Hamilton MA Headmaster'

The salary was £250 and the Headmaster was allowed £25 for 'coals and cleaning'. Mr. C. J. Berry was appointed as his assistant (£100), the Rev. Jeremiah Coombes as Under Master (£100), Mr. John Vaughan as Usher (£80), Mr. G. Burrowes as his assistant (£70), and Mr. C. Smith for drawing (£30, part-time).

The School appears to have got off to a flourishing start. There was soon an orchestra and a dramatic society; the cadet corps was more than 100 strong by 1864. The Goldsmiths were content: they had presented a library of more than 800 volumes, and their Chaplain, the Rev. J. H. Ward, was the Examiner in 1861. There were difficulties here and there, but they were easily solved: 'The Stone grids in the Garden beneath the windows of the Head Master's Dwelling House allowing the escape of an Effluvium from the Main Sewer were ordered to be rectified' in June 1862; and a year later the Trustees heard from the Headmaster: 'that in order to provide for the comfort of the Trustees at their meetings, I am obliged to leave my Study, my only sitting room, without a chair'. The Trustees, optimistically, bought fourteen chairs; there was never a meeting when all fourteen were required!

During 1864 the Schools Inquiry Commission, set up by Parliament to examine and report on the condition of the ancient foundations, visited the School. Its Report was published in 1867 and makes fascinating reading. There were then 172 pupils in the School, all 'middle class' as the Report says, including seven boarders in the Headmaster's house. There were seven masters, offering a classical education in the Upper School (130 pupils) and a commercial in the Lower. The endowment was £307 a year: £300 from the Goldsmiths, and £7 interest on gifts of £100 from Alderman Ephraim Hallam and £50 from Dr. Edwin Rayner providing annual prizes. The School was criticised for not having sent any pupils on to University for some years – not surprising, in view of the cessation of the Goldsmiths' £50 Exhibitions.

When one considers that of the 782 endowed schools investigated by the Commission, only about forty were described as 'flourishing and efficient', it is clear that the School was indeed prospering. It seems that Hamilton received independent confirmation of how good the School was. At the end of 1866 he had asked the Governors for a testimonial, as he was applying for a post in the Midlands:

'The Trustees of the Stockport Grammar and Free School, having taken into consideration an application by the Rev. C. G. Hamilton, MA, for a

Testimonial as a Candidate for the Headmaster-ship of the Birmingham and Edgbaston Proprietary School, feel that while they should be sorry to part with services so valuable to their own school, they cannot, in justice to him, refuse him the opportunity of improving his position, and they cordially wish him that success to which, both from ability and experience, he is so eminently entitled.'

Having actually visited the Birmingham school, however, Hamilton decided not to move. The Commission's Report also suggested that the 'commercial' side at Stockport should be expanded, but this was only partially acted upon, when in 1869 Greek was made a voluntary subject and Natural Philosophy was introduced as a substitute for Pure Mathematics. As the Examiner put it:

'Though Greek ought to be preferred to Latin as an instrument of education, and Trigonometry is better than Natural Philosophy, yet in this age and neighbourhood due regard must be paid to the demands which trade and commerce make upon boys immediately after they have left the school. In this respect, Latin and Mechanics are useful.'

However by 1873 the Examiner was 'very glad to find that Greek, one of the highest elements of a perfect education, is again included in the subjects taught in the School'.

Though the School was successful on the academic side, it was not proving to be financially worthwhile, and the establishment of Public Elementary Schools by the 1870 Education Act did nothing to help. The School was kept afloat by the endowments and by the generosity of the Trustees. By 1872 the amount owed to the Trustees was £944 4 10d, and no amount of financial juggling – such as paying the staff a small fixed stipend plus so much for each pupil – could apparently work.[2]

Yet the School managed to struggle on. Year by year the Examiners commended the high quality of the work that was done, and bemoaned the lack of Exhibitions to take successful scholars on to University. From 1877, to receive a little more income, the School accepted School Board Foundationers, of whom the first was John Dunville. But by 1878 matters had reached the stage where it was necessary to revise the Statutes, in an attempt to halt the decline in numbers. 1879 was occupied by great debates on a new Scheme of Management for the School, with little immediate result, apart from the founding of a £40 scholarship for University entrants. This was endowed by the executors of the late John Benjamin Smith, Member of Parliament for Stockport between 1852 and 1874, and is still awarded annually, though it is now merely a prize. The first recipient of the original scholarship was Norcross Burrowes in 1880, who went on to graduate from the Victoria University of Manchester in 1884.

In June 1880, in the midst of the great debates, the School was examined as usual:

'[There is] little to be said but in the way of commendation. The teaching is just as accurate and painstaking and thorough as I have found in previous years. The weak point in the school is due to the folly of parents who remove their sons from the school at too early an age. It is not fair to your able Headmaster and his assistants; it is not fair to the foundation of Sir Edmond Shaa; it is not fair to the boys that they should be taken away from the school at so early an age.'[3]

The new Scheme, having been sanctioned by the Charity Commissioners, was finally approved by the Queen on 15th July 1881. It had two main effects, the first of which was beneficial, in that the

The accounts for 1872 – with Upper School fees at £7 and Lower at £3 10s – are informative:

INCOME				EXPENDITURE			
				Head Master – allowance	50	0	0
				half Upper fees	329	0	0
				Under Master – allowance	90	0	0
				all Lower fees	77	0	0
Upper School fees	658	0	0	1st Assistant – salary	100	0	0
Lower School fees	77	0	0	capitation	44	0	0
Goldsmiths' grant	300	0	0	2nd Assistant – salary	80	0	0
Dr. Rayner's prize	2	9	3	capitation	22	0	0
Ald. Hallam's prize	4	18	6	French & German Master	50	0	0
Mr. Shipman's prize	1	0	0	Drawing Master	30	0	0
				Trustees' Expenditure	171	7	9
TOTAL	£1043	7	9	TOTAL	£1043	7	9

School gained a certain measure of independence from the Town Council, for various other public bodies were invited to nominate Governors. One of these, intriguingly, was the non-existent Board of Magistrates for the Petty Sessions of Heaton Norris: the Charity Commissioners had been rather concerned, during the drafting of the Scheme, that letters addressed to this body were never answered, but pressed on with its inclusion regardless. The effects of the error were not rectified until 1888, when the Commissioners agreed that the vacant appointment should be filled by a nominee from 'the Magistrates for Lancashire meeting at Manchester and qualified as ex officio Poor Law Guardians of the Board of Guardians for the Union of Stockport.'

The second effect was unfortunate. Since the troubles of 1860, the Goldsmiths had paid the £300 a year endowment to the School but had shunned any further involvement. Now they were offered the chance to nominate a Governor; this they declined, understandably in view of what had happened. But the existence of the offer – however it arose – reminded the town of what once had been a great benefit, and the Company of what had become a great burden, which it had no wish to assume again, however indirectly.

Like all new schemes or revisions of old ones, this New Scheme was greeted with enthusiasm. The first meeting of the Governors was held on 12th August 1881 and the seven present decided to appoint Mr. Edward Walmsley to the Chair before proceeding to make arrangements for a Clerk, to deal with the accounts (for which proper books were now to be kept), and to inspect the Deeds of the School with the Town Clerk. A pressing necessity was to publish the Scheme, and they ordered the printing of 300 copies, to be sold at 6d each. As far as the School was concerned, the Headmaster (reappointed) was requested to purchase books and stationery, to be sold to the pupils, and 'pens, ink, inkpots, and indiarubber' which were to be supplied free of charge. Innovations in the curriculum included vocal music and Natural Science (though lectures on Geology, Chemistry, and Zoology had been arranged since as early as 1871).

The enthusiasm of the Governors was short-lived. Only three attended the next meeting on 21st September, at which it was resolved to take steps to reduce the quorum from five to three, and the meeting adjourned; two weeks later, however, steps had not been taken – in the absence of a quorum, of course, it was impossible – and the meeting had again to be adjourned with only four present. Those who had attended informed their colleagues of the fact – and they took the hint. Six

attended on 26th October: another resigned by letter (he 'did not have the time to attend meetings'!) The reduction in the quorum was not pressed.

There was the novelty of a Teacher of Singing and a Science Lecturer (each at 10/6d a lesson). The Governors' commitment to the new scientific revolution is perhaps summed up in the concluding paragraph of the Minutes:

'Some discussion took place respecting the provision of Science teaching, but nothing much was done.'[4]

The last meeting of the year took place on 15th December. The accounts were approved and it was moved that 'a box be obtained for the Custody of the Deeds, & be lettered "Stockport Grammar School" '. There were 91 boys in the School, and the decline in numbers was to continue.

1882 began with a fresh wave of enthusiasm. No fewer than eleven Governors attended the first meeting on 15th March, which resolved to have quarterly accounts, and quarterly reports from the Headmaster. The question of scientific education was brought up again later, this time in a letter from the Mayor, Mr. James Leigh, who offered £40 or £50 from his own pocket for furnishing a laboratory. The matter remained 'under consideration' – perhaps inevitably, as the precarious financial position of the School continued to keep its very existence at stake. The Examiner's Report was, as usual, good. The School was found to be in 'good working order' with 'much to praise and little to blame'. There were five successes in the Oxford Local Examinations, well up to standard. The boys' physical welfare was by no means neglected: the Headmaster was pleased to accept 'what is called, I believe, a wrestling bar, i.e. a horizontal bar with suitable uprights' for the playground from Mr. Emery of Stepping Hill.

1883 began in crisis, for Hamilton was taken seriously ill, and the Governors had to make special arrangements, both to have the School opened for the beginning of term and to arrange a substitute master. The vacancy was filled first by the Rev. H. Cottam, Rector of St. Mary's, Crumpsall, who knew the school well, having been one of the Annual Examiners and having stood in during a previous illness of Hamilton's in 1875. The Rector was put in charge for a fortnight to begin with, but when there was no improvement in Hamilton it was decided to investigate the possibility of appointing a proper substitute. One was soon found and at a special meeting of the Governors on 26th February Mr. C. G. Higginson, a graduate of the University of London, was appointed at a salary of £5 a week, to be paid by Hamilton.

Cottam suggested that he too should have been paid for his fortnight's service, but the Governors replied that they were under the impression that 'his services had been tendered on behalf of and as the personal friend of Mr. Hamilton'. In March, however, they relented and – perhaps persuaded by the convalescent Hamilton – agreed to pay him eight guineas.

The Governors were not simply parsimonious: in truth they continued to be deeply concerned about the financial state of the School. In April they decided to devote no more than £10, in addition to the income from bequests, for prizes, and to make a 'direct and formal' application to the Goldsmiths for some assistance. The Minutes of the meeting on 20th June record, in characteristically brief fashion: 'The state of the finances was under discussion for some time . . .', but there was no doubt about 'the serious financial condition of the establishment'.

Some continued to have confidence. Higginson, crowning his 'busy life among the Stockport boys' ventured to make some comments to the Governors in a letter on 14th June, 'not through any belief that, in your present position in financial and other matters, you can act upon them soon; but when and if the ability comes'. The accommodation – four rooms, including the Headmaster's dining-room, for four masters – was ample, even if the ventilation left something to be desired. What was wrong lay really with the time-tabling of the School: problems of organization and curriculum. The problem of organization went back to the 1881 Scheme which Higginson – 'If I understood that Scheme at all' – took to mean that the two schools (Upper and Lower) were to be united absolutely into one. But this was impossible, so long as fees were based on age rather than grade. A smooth progression from Lower to Upper became impossible, and fees were as jumbled as subjects.

In the curriculum there were problems concerning two subjects. Latin was optional, and paid for separately, in the Lower School, but compulsory and included in the fees in the Upper. Naturally – for reasons of economy – some boys were deterred from progressing and continued in the Lower School, wasting their time. A new subject was drawing pupils away from the top of the School: by neglecting the proper provision of scientific education.

'how terribly the work of the Sixth Form is cut up during the year by the three mornings and one afternoon per week that our boys spend in attending Dr. Roscoe's Chymistry [sic] classes in Manchester.'

Higginson set the Governors an ironical choice: send the boys to Manchester deliberately or provide in Stockport 'all the subjects necessary for the Matriculation'.

The parents did not escape criticism: 'the attendance of many of the boys was very far from satisfactory, parents having largely contracted habits of great laxity in absenting their children for trifling reasons'. These criticisms were echoed by that year's Examiner, Mr. G. E. Hignett of Brasenose College, Oxford, in his Report. His examination was something of a novelty, as it was conducted by means of written papers and not orally, as had been the case in the past. Thus, a clearer picture of each boy's knowledge of each subject could be assessed, and in any case 'the prizes should be governed by the year's work, not one day's'.

Despite the happy applause of Speech Day on 20th June, the Governors were perhaps thinking ahead to their next meeting, a fortnight away, 'respecting the financial position of the School'. A 'conversation' – again the minutes are terse – took place and the meeting was adjourned until the next Monday. Eight now attended instead of five, and Mr. James Leigh proposed:

'that it is desirable that before anything is done as to interfere in the internal arrangement of the School, that application be made to the Goldsmiths' Company for an additional grant.' Leigh travelled to London to meet the Goldsmiths later in July, but 'found them not at home'.

September's quarterly meeting brought the bad news of a fall in the number of boys – from 82 to 69 in a year – and a suggestion from the Headmaster that the year should be arranged in three terms – as was elsewhere by then more usual – instead of in four quarters. The Governors referred back to Hamilton the matter of terms and of advertisements giving notice of the change, and with that was concluded the business of the last quarter of quartered years at the School. In November it was resolved to adopt terms, as from January 1884. There still remained the financial plight. Mr. Walter Prideaux, the Clerk to the Goldsmiths' Company, wrote to the Governors on 22nd November, leaving little doubt about the attitude of the Company:

'[The transfer in 1860] between the Goldsmiths' Company and the Corporation was carried through with the most perfect agreement and accord.'
'The Corporation at that time felt that the offer made to them was an act of great liberality, and accepted it with a clear understanding that the

connection between the Goldsmiths' Company and the School (excepting the large annual endowment of £290 which the Company agreed to pay was concerned) was at an end. Therefore in 1879 when the Company were solicited by the Charity Commissioners to nominate some of the Governors under the new Scheme they declined to do so. The Corporation expressed their satisfaction with the endowment and their conviction that it would be ample for the purposes of the School. Since then the population of Stockport has increased and, no doubt, its wealth has increased also, and it certainly seems extraordinary that the School now should be an entire failure. It would almost seem that by the establishment of Elementary Schools and of the Manchester Grammar School, the necessity for the Stockport School has been superseded, but, if that be not so, it is extraordinary that the inhabitants of Stockport are unwilling or unable to aid the institution.'

So that was that. Leigh and Prideaux had also corresponded privately, and got on well together. The former agreed 'that Gurney had been a very difficult person to manage and was probably the source of all the mischief'. But it was still the case that with respect to the School 'now it is not a credit but a disgrace to us'.

During the following months the School managed to carry on, but the atmosphere must have been one of great despondency. Hope, however, was provided by the offer of a gift of £1,000 from Alderman Ephraim Hallam, to provide leaving scholarships for boys to go on to University. But the over-riding problem was really to ensure that there would continue to be a School for boys to progress from. As Hamilton noted:

'If nothing has yet been settled with regard to Ald. Hallam's gift of a thousand pounds, it seems to me well worth considering whether it would not be more advantageous to the School to endow a "Hallam Lectureship in Natural Science" than to found a scholarship. Another thousand pounds, if it could be obtained, would perhaps be sufficient for the building of a small Laboratory, and for the cleaning and repairs so urgently required both in the Schoolrooms and in the School house.'

Numbers declined further during 1885: by December there were only 57 pupils. At the summer Examination it had been suggested that

'A great impetus would be given to this School if 10 Exhibitions of £10 each and 10 of £5 each could be offered for competition to boys attending the elementary schools of Stockport.'

Hallam's generous gift providing leaving scholarships was finally accepted, and he himself became a Governor in October 1885. The first meeting of 1886 was specially convened to pay tribute to the work of the late Mr. Lister Ives, Under Master since Coombes had left in 1862, and to express sympathy to Mrs. Ives and her daughter. They soon had to leave the School Cottage where they had lived, but they were granted a payment of £5 for 'the bath and fittings' left in the cottage, which was quickly rented out to provide a valuable £35 a year of extra income.

Early in 1887 the Governors decided that the decline in numbers had gone far enough (though in fact it went on still further). There were only fourteen pupils in the Upper School, and thirty in the Lower, and a voluminous correspondence with the Charity Commissioners now commenced. The minutes of the January meeting record:

'That the Rev. C. G. Hamilton having at the suggestion of the Governors agreed to retire from the Headmastership on a pension, the Governors beg respectfully to suggest £150 per annum as such pension, and ask the advice of the Charity Commissioners on the subject.'

The Commissioners enquired how and why would the pension be paid, and the Governors explained that Hamilton was now 67, had been Headmaster for 27 years, and although not then in bad health had two or three years previously had a serious illness, and was not considered equal to the work. The pension of £150 was to be paid out of the Goldsmiths' endowment of £290. The Commissioners pondered. The Governors wrote again, to say that they considered that the School's present difficulties and deficit of £170 6 4d were due to the introduction of the previous Scheme (by then only six years old!) and to the establishment of Higher Grade Schools in connection with Elementary Schools. The average attendance at the Grammar School in the six years to 1881 was 138, but in 1882–86, 78. Of the 1,500 scholars on the roll at St. Thomas's Elementary School, no fewer than 240 were in the Higher Grade classes. The Higher Grade Schools charged only 9d a week, and the Grammar School fees were now £9 a year, or more than four times as great.

NADIR AND REBIRTH

In the midst of these negotiations, the Committee of the proposed new Technical School approached the Governors to buy a part of the Grammar School playground as the site for their new building. As discussions proceeded, the sale of the land became tied to the payment of Hamilton's pension, for the Charity Commissioners decided that if the land could be sold for a chief rent of £58 10 0d [£4 per cent of its market value], then the pension could be £125 – but £50 of that would have to come from the salary of the new Headmaster! Negotiations continued, and advertisements for the new Headmaster attracted 123 candidates. Six were interviewed, and eventually the Rev. William Alfred Pemberton, an Oxford graduate, was appointed, as from 1st January 1888. Hamilton returned full-time to the ministry, and died as Vicar of St. Chad's, Handforth, on 10th March 1895.

The programme for the December 1877 production.

One other important change took place before the end of the year, the appointment of Mr. J. W. Johnston as Clerk to the Governors. This was the beginning of a family association with the School which was to last until 1942, when his son, who succeeded him in 1898, retired. Johnston was soon deep in correspondence with Mr. Russell Coppock, Solicitor to the Technical School Committee, Old Boy, and son of Major Coppock, concerning the purchase of the land. The final Governors' meeting of 1887 marked the School's nadir – five Upper School pupils and 17 in the Lower, and Pemberton signed the Minute Book accepting his new position. What must his thoughts have been? Whatever they were, his appointment seems to have transformed the School. Within four months of his coming, numbers had risen to 27; within seven, there were 53, and he was authorized to take on an assistant from September. The Annual Examination was postponed until December, because of the large number of new pupils. A new atmosphere – tentative hope replacing darkest gloom – spurred the Governors. The sale of the land to the Technical School went through (the Foundation Stone was laid on 8th September 1888) and a new playground for the School was made for the grand sum of £97. Furthermore,

---

STOCKPORT GRAMMAR SCHOOL.

Saturday Evening, December 22, 1877.

PART I—
SHAKESPEARE'S TRAGEDY:
"KING RICHARD THE II."
Curtailed and arranged expressly for this occasion.

DRAMATIS PERSONÆ:

King Richard the II	F. W. SHAWCROSS
John of Gaunt, Duke of Lancaster } uncles to Duke of York } the king.	W. H. PAGE H. HAWKINS
Duke of Aumerle, son to the Duke of York	S. HUNT
Henry Bolingbroke, Duke of Hereford, son to John of Gaunt and afterwards Henry IV	E. A. CROMPTON
Thomas Mowbray, Duke of Norfolk	R. PEIRCE
Earl of Salisbury	H. W. OLDHAM
Bushy } Bagot } servants to King Richard Green }	E. J. CHEETHAM E. CHEETHAM N. BURROWS
Earl of Northumberland	J. G. WARD
Henry Percy, his son	S. B. CHEETHAM
Bishop of Carlisle	J. BALE
Sir Stephen Scroop	H. ROSCOE
Sir Pierce of Exton	R. HOWARD
Keeper of Prison	T. H. CHATTERTON
Groom	H. CHALONER
Servants }	E. J. SHAWCROSS S. MOSS
Soldiers }	G. PARKES W. JOWETT J. LOMAX W. H. CROSS

Interval of Fifteen Minutes.

PART II—
"Raising the Wind."
A Farce in One Act, by James Kenney.

DRAMATIS PERSONÆ:

Plainway	J. G. WARD
Fainwould	W. H. PAGE
Jeremy Diddler	R. PEIRCE
Sam	H. HAWKINS
Richard	N. BURROWS
Waiter	E. CHEETHAM
John, servant to Plainway	S. HUNT
Peggy	E. A. CROMPTON
Miss Laurelia Durable	H. ROSCOE

GOD SAVE THE QUEEN.

The Music, selected from the works of Mozart and Beethoven, will be under the direction of Mr. J. H. SMITH.

'The Governors inspected the School building and the darkness of the large room having been a frequent source of complaint and of expense in the use of gas [for lighting], Captain Sykes offered at his own cost to employ an architect and have the windows lowered to a suitable height.'

And £43 10 0d was spent on new desks, in spite of an overdraft of £212 16 3d! The worst seemed to be over: by the end of the Summer Term in 1889, numbers had risen to 89, and Pemberton was pleased to report that 'there has been no caning this term'. He was allowed another £100 for masters (bringing the total to £350 a year).

Captain Sykes

'suggested that arrangements should be made under which the Technical School should work in co-operation with the Grammar School. The Headmaster expressed his concurrence with the suggestion as the Technical School could supply subjects of instruction not dealt with at a Grammar School, and stated that he had under consideration a scheme as to classes and fees having this object in view.'

The Greek Street building at the turn of the century. Notice the lengthening of the windows to provide more light: this work had been carried out in the late 1880s at the expense of Captain Sykes, Chairman of Governors. In the background is the Technical College, built in 1888/9 on land bought from the School.
[Reproduced by permission of the Metropolitan Borough of Stockport.]

By the end of the year numbers had risen still further to 109, and an Old Boys' Association had been formed. Co-operation with the Technical School extended to letting the Grammar School out for evening lectures at a fee of two guineas per lecture. The Examiner's Report for 1890 stated:

'The work and discipline in the School seem to improve term by term – yet there is room for greater improvement if some parents would be a little less indulgent in giving excuses for their boys for not having prepared their work.'

During the early 1890s numbers settled at about 120, and academic progress was maintained.[1] In 1892 the Headmaster could announce that 'twice as many honours and distinctions and just over twice as many certificates as last year have been gained.

The School is first of all Grammar Schools in Cheshire in these Cambridge examinations'. Yet the Examiner noted that in 'History Form 4 were bad. They knew hardly anything about such an important subject as Magna Carta'.

During 1893 Captain Sykes became Chairman of Governors, and found himself almost immediately contributing to the 'substantial repairs' needed to the buildings. Other Governors – notably Aldermen Hallam and Leigh – also gave generously, but there were always problems, as Colonel Wilkinson, a Governor for many years, noted acerbically:

'The roof did not actually leak very much before it was taken in hand to be repaired; but is now reported to be in need of more repairs.' He advised finishing with the architect in Manchester and 'getting a local man in'.

Meanwhile the Goldsmiths were taking steps finally to sever their connection with the School. Intimation had been received during the previous year that they were considering paying over to the Official Trustee of Charitable Funds the sum of £12,000, the interest on which would be sufficient to maintain their endowment of £300. The Charity Commissioners, involved once again, enquired about a sum of £500 which the Company had agreed to pay in 1881 'in aid of the improvements required'. In view of the passage of time, the Goldsmiths increased this amount to £575, and requested that the School should remove from the buildings the stone inscriptions bearing witness to their former patronage. This was done, and a connection which had existed unbroken for more than four centuries was at an end.

The 1894 Scheme brought in new Governors to represent the Cheshire and Lancashire County Councils and Owens College in Manchester, since 1880 a constituent college of the Victoria University. There were to be three more co-opted Governors, to be appointed for a term of five years, but none was to be appointed until the original 'life' Governors gave up their seats. The first representative of the College was the Beyer Professor of Mathematics there, Horace Lamb, an Old Boy and first President of the Old Boys' Association. He had been a pupil back in the days of Gurney and Hamilton, and in 1867 had won the Prizes in Greek, Latin, English, and Mathematics. The Examiner had commented:

'I ought not to omit to recommend to your favourable attention Horace Lamb. He is a boy of very good promise and will I have no doubt (if he continues to work steadily) do credit to the School.'

Later in that year he had taught for seven weeks in the school (a replacement master could not start immediately) and had been paid £7. In 1868 he was awarded a Minor Entrance Scholarship to Cambridge, and the School celebrated with an extra holiday on 8th May. Prize Day in December 1894 was novel in that Mrs. Sykes presented the prizes: the Clerk to the Governors had suggested 'as ladies were now taking such a prominent place in everything, they should ask a lady to present the prizes'.

Relations between the School and the Corporation were somewhat strained during the 1890s. There was a clear feeling on the part of some Councillors that, since the School was no longer under their sole control and since they now had their own Technical School to worry about (they had been responsible for its organization and financing from March 1892), they need no longer be too concerned about the Grammar School. This was despite the fact that many of the Councillors were also Governors. For instance, the Borough Surveyor wrote to ask for repairs to be made to the wall between the School and Greek Street: he was politely but firmly informed that the wall was not dangerous, 'having been in that condition for twenty years'!

The Headmaster of the Technical School, Mr. R. J. Brown, wrote to enquire if some more of the playground could be bought, but the price requested – £37 10s for 1,500 square yards – was 'too much'. Other schemes for co-operation between the two schools also foundered. Pemberton was instructed to confer with Brown

'with the view to promoting the co-operation of the two schools and the possibility of avoiding the teaching subjects in the two schools having a tendency to overlap and so bringing the two schools more fully in accord with the requirements of the town.'

The meeting was not a success: its

'only result seemed to shew that the parents of Stockport families preferred a cheap commercial education to a more expensive higher intellectual one and that the latter was necessarily more costly and that the Grammar School fees could not possibly be reduced to the level of the Technical School fees, that School being subsidised by Excise Duties and Government Grants to the amount of double the fees received from Scholars.'

Agreement was however reached on selling the Grammar School Cottage and its land to the Technical School Committee, and the sale went through in 1900 for £1,125. Pemberton also started classes in book-keeping and shorthand, in response to parents' answers to a questionnaire. The number of boys fluctuated around 100, but the School at last seemed to have become viable, a credit balance appearing in the accounts for the first time. Hamilton's death in 1895 brought the Headmaster a rise in Salary to £150, as he no longer had to fund his predecessor's pension. Gratuities were paid to Mrs. Pemberton and also to Mrs. Cossart, whose husband had taught Modern Languages for 25 years, and one of £100 was offered to Johnston the Clerk when he retired, but he declined.

Academically the School and its pupils prospered. There were Credits and Distinctions in the Matriculation lists each year, but the outstanding name of this period is undoubtedly that of Maurice Powicke, who was born in 1879, the eldest son of the Congregational Minister in Romiley. He entered the School in 1893 and, on leaving in 1896 – having obtained a first class in the London Matriculation the previous December – was awarded the John Benjamin Smith Exhibition to pursue his studies at Manchester. By 1899, having collected almost every available Prize and Exhibition there, he had obtained a First Class Honours degree in History at the London Examination, and his School Exhibition was extended to take him to Balliol College, Oxford, where he obtained a further First Class in History in 1903.

The School was unfortunate to lose two of its most hardworking Governors within the space of seven months. Colonel Wilkinson, who died in October 1900, had been on the Board for 22 years. A typical Victorian gentleman of enormous energy and breadth of interest, he had combined the office with being a Guardian of the Poor, a Magistrate, a Musician of some repute, working for Stockport Sunday School and the Infirmary, and had also been Chairman of the short-lived Stockport School Board in the 1870s. The other loss was that of the Chairman himself, Captain Sykes, who died on 25th April 1901. His interests and activities had coincided with and exceeded even those of the Colonel, for he was heavily involved in the family business too. Shortly before his death he had been pleased to see his son, Major Alan Sykes, also later to be Chairman, appointed to the Board.

In his will Captain Sykes left the School £1,000, and his son proposed that it be used to build an extra classroom. This was speedily agreed, but the Headmaster was not able to see it in use himself, for in July 1902 he announced to the Governors that he had been offered – and intended to accept – a small country living, a 'less onerous position'. This turned out to be that of St. Michael's, the Parish Church of Mottram in Longdendale – the stone tower of which church

Sir Edmond Shaa had caused to be erected by the terms of his will.

These two coats of arms from the Greek Street building are preserved at Buxton Road. Sir Edmond's are built into the wall of Shaa House, the Headmaster's residence; the Goldsmiths' are below the modern Hall.

DANIELS

From the seven candidates eventually interviewed for the vacant headmastership, Mr. Alfred Edward Daniels was appointed. Daniels, the first layman to become Headmaster of Stockport Grammar School, was a Cambridge graduate and a first-class Mathematician (fifth Wrangler in 1891), and had previously been Head of Physics and Head of Mathematics at Nottingham High School. The appointment of a scientist to the post was clearly significant, in view of past experiences. The salary was £150 a year, together with a capitation fee of £3 for each boy. A further £375 was allowed him for assistants, and £52 for a 'Caretaker, heating, cleaning, coal, and coke'. There were 54 pupils in the Upper School and 42 in the Lower.

One of the earliest School Photographs, from about 1910, showing Headmaster Daniels (front row, fifth from right), his teaching staff, and boys.

In his first Report to the Governors, Daniels noted that it was difficult to teach three languages, and so he had made German alternative to Latin in the Upper School, and French alternative in the Lower. 'For boys who do not take shorthand, I have introduced the subject of Measurement, in which boys are carefully taught the use of the scale, protractor, and vernier. In the course of the next term or so I hope to develop this subject into elementary Mechanics and Physics. The boys take a great interest in this Subject and the work done will be of vital use to such as afterwards become Engineers, Surveyors, Scientists, etc.' The significant point here was that if four hours each week were devoted to the teaching of Science, the School would become eligible for a grant of £150 a year, under a scheme recently introduced by the newly-created Board of Education.

The Board had been set up according to the provisions of the 1902 Education Act, which also created Local Education Authorities. The School applied to the Board for recognition as a Secondary School, and this was duly granted. Thus ended the Annual Examination, as the Board conducted its own inspections. Daniels had already condemned the publication of the Examiner's Report as a 'very unusual practice in Secondary Schools with nothing to commend it'.

But the new Headmaster did not try to turn the School into a Technical School, with a full science curriculum. He recognized that

'in a school such as ours where the teaching has distinct literary and mathematical pretensions and in which school hours are shorter than is the case in some parts of the country there is not, under present conditions, sufficient time for the proper development of both subjects; and experts are nearly unanimous in the opinion that Physics affords a better intellectual training than Chemistry, and the expense and risk in maintaining a Physical Laboratory is also distinctly less.'

He also sought advice on drill from a Capt. Bradshaw, 'to improve the bearing and physical condition of the boys', and soon fifty pupils had joined the School Cricket Club, practising regularly on Stockport Cricket Club's ground. This proved to be an unsatisfactory arrangement, and with the help of the Old Boys' Association a four-acre field in Adswood was purchased. Daniels bought a small Pavilion, and a groundsman was engaged at £1 4 0d a week. By 1909 a stable had been erected (costing £14) for the horse (£3) which pulled the roller over the field.

The Headmaster's ideas on discipline seem to have been ahead of the times. During early 1904 a 'Morris Tube Range' (like a shooting gallery) was erected, and he noted:

'I shall only allow those boys to use the range who have attained considerable proficiency in their physical exercises and drill; and all shooting will be carried on under the strictest supervision. I may say that the above "idea" belongs to my system of controlling the boys by "influence" rather than by the "cane". Ill-behaved boys are denied privileges granted to well-conducted boys.'[1]

By the end of the year there were 79 boys in the three Senior forms, and 62 in the two Junior. Daniels proposed to add two forms to the Senior, one at the top and one at the bottom, and to take on another master. The fees were set at £6 for the Junior Department and £10 for the Senior; and there was to be no age differentiation in future. Building work at the School included the new Sykes classroom and the re-laying of the floor in the large hall; outside, when a double tram track was laid in Greek Street in 1905, the Governors paid £100 to have 60 yards of wooden blocks (instead of stone setts) put down, to lessen the noise from the street.

Ironically, in view of what had happened fifty years earlier, it was now the School's success which precipitated the next crisis. By 1910 there were 155 pupils on the roll; although this was only five more than that for which the original buildings had been designed, and there was now also the extra Sykes classroom, the Board of Education indicated that there was serious overcrowding and something would have to be done: the School fell considerably short of modern standards, and unless the Governors could provide suitable accommodation, the grant would not be paid after July 1915. There was no room to expand satisfactorily at Greek Street, especially because of the loss of land sold to the Technical School for its building and subsequent expansion. The only solution was to move.

Six sites were shortlisted for the new buildings. One, in Heaton Norris, was not seriously considered, as that area was thought to be too near to Manchester Grammar School. Two others were near the Crown Inn on Buxton Road in Great Moor: one, behind the Inn, was found to be too near to Stepping Hill Hospital, and the other, opposite the Inn and between Buxton Road and Dialstone Lane, was not quite large enough. The same was true of the available part of the Highfield House estate in Davenport: another drawback here was the distance from any tram route. The remaining two sites were the Mile End Hall estate, where Stockport School now stands, and the place eventually chosen and now occupied by the School, the Bramhall Lodge estate, then owned by Mr. Alfred Bell, a member of the well-known local brewing family. The proximity of the London & North Western Railway station at Davenport, together with the easy access from it to the School, was the deciding factor between these last two.

Negotiations were started to purchase the site, and the London architects Spalding and Spalding were commissioned to draw up the plans. The site was quickly bought, the plans were quickly prepared; but the Board of Education was unhappy about the cost – £32,000 – and suggested economies. The proposed swimming pool fell victim and £2,000 was saved. The Board was also somewhat worried about the style of the buildings, thinking it rather ornate for a mere school. The Governors however were resolved that

'it was desirable that the buildings to be erected should be of a character suitable for a Grammar School and not limited to those of an ordinary Secondary School and that the position be fully reported to the Educational Charities in the Town.'

These responded magnificently. The Ephraim Hallam Charity promised £18,500, and a further £4,000 was donated while the School was being built; £2,000 came from the Brownell Charity; Mr.

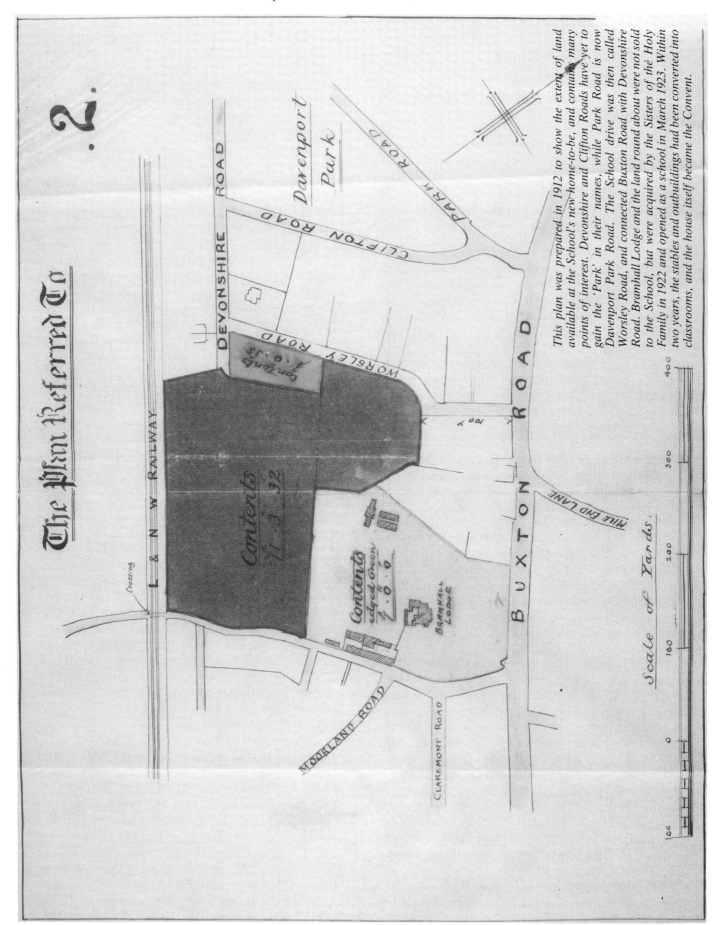

The Plan Referred To

This plan was prepared in 1912 to show the extent of land available at the School's new home-to-be, and contains many points of interest. Devonshire and Clifton Roads have yet to gain the 'Park' in their names, while Park Road is now Davenport Park Road. The School drive was then called Worsley Road, and connected Buxton Road with Devonshire Road. Bramhall Lodge and the land round about were not sold to the School, but were acquired by the Sisters of the Holy Family in 1922 and opened as a school in March 1923. Within two years, the stables and outbuildings had been converted into classrooms, and the house itself became the Convent.

Publicity Material from Spalding and Theakston, 1914. Notice the reference to the projected Swimming Bath: the lower courses of the outside wall of the Gymnasium were in fact tiled, in case it should ever be built.
[Reproduced by permission of the Worshipful Company of Goldsmiths.]

THE NEW STOCKPORT GRAMMAR SCHOOL

is in course of erection at Davenport. The site is approached from Buxton Road by a private road and contains eleven acres of almost level ground on which are a few fine old trees. It is an ideal site for the purpose.

Full advantage has been taken of the opportunity of facing the principal facade so that it can be seen from the main line of the London and North-Western Railway, which bounds the site on the south-west. The Principal Entrance is planned on the central axis of the main block, and is approached from the terrace in front overlooking the playing fields. A Collegiate type of plan has been adopted, the class rooms and principals' rooms being arranged round a central quadrangle. The Great Hall lies on the central axis of the quadrangle and principal facade and is directly approached from the Main Entrance and forms one side of the quadrangle.

The scholars will enter the school buildings by a special entrance gateway under the tower, The Sergeant's Room is arranged adjoining this entrance and entirely commanding it.

Accommodation will be provided for 250 scholars and includes every requirement for a Modern Grammar School. On the Ground Floor there will be five class rooms, each accommodating twenty-four students, and on the first floor five class rooms, accommodating the same number. There will also be two division rooms, each accommodating fifteen students, and these rooms will be used for special subject classes or advanced study.

The Science and Art Departments are arranged on the first floor entirely separated from the other rooms. The Science Department will comprise two laboratories, preparation and balance rooms for advanced science, and a lecture room. A large studio lighted from the north will be provided for art students.

On the ground floor provision will be made for a large dining room for the use of day boarders, with service kitchens adjoining.

The Headmaster's Room will be placed near to the platform of the Great Hall and the Governors' Room. The Library will be in a quiet position and a Common Room for the use of the Masters is to be provided.

The Great Hall will be 59 feet long by 30 feet wide, and will be approached from all the corridors and the quadrangle. This arrangement not only allows easy assembly but in the case of emergency the Hall can be rapidly cleared. A large platform is arranged at the northern end of the Hall and a space will be provided at the southern end for an organ. The Hall will be lighted by three large mullioned bay windows overlooking the quadrangle and will be panelled in oak. The plaster ceiling, segmental in form, supported with Doric pilasters and enriched cornices, will be panelled with fibrous plaster enrichments and mouldings. Facing the windows at the first floor level three balconies are being arranged projecting into the Hall and finished in oak.

There will be a large Gymnasium with gallery for visitors, and a Swimming Bath, which it is intended to build in the near future, has been included in laying out the scheme.

Cloak and Lavatory accommodation will be arranged in accordance with the Board of Education requirements for each student.

Adjoining the exercise ground four fives courts have been arranged and the play in these courts can be watched from the terrace. From this terrace a good view of the playing fields will be obtained and visitors will have ample accommodation for viewing the play which should prove an attraction on match days.

A small house is to be provided for the accommodation of the caretaker, arranged in connection with the service kitchen of the dining room.

Accommodation for scholars' cycles will be provided at the entrance gates.

The building throughout will be heated with hot water.

The external elevations will be finished in red brick and stone and the roofing in green slating. Over the Main Entrance there will be four carved panels, representing the history of the school from the date of its foundation in 1487.

The construction throughout will be fire-resisting, and all appliances and fittings of the latest modern type.

The Architects, Mr. Reginald H. Spalding, F.R.I.B.A., and Mr. Ernest G. Theakston, F.R.I.B.A., of 36 and 37, King Street, London, E.C., expect to have the work completed in the summer of 1915. The Contractors are Messrs. Daniel Eadie & Co., of Stockport.

The opening ceremony of the new School at Buxton Road took place on Saturday 29th January 1916. The builder, Mr. Daniel Eadie, is second from left on the front row; next is Mr. Joel Wainwright; then Mr. Henry Bell (a Governor), Colonel Dixon (Chairman of Cheshire County Council, who performed the actual opening), Dr. Edwin Rayner (Chairman of Governors), Mr. A. E. Daniels (Headmaster), and Mr. W. Johnston (Clerk to the Governors). Behind Mr. Bell is Professor Lamb (in the hat), and behind Dr. Rayner and the Headmaster is Colonel Sykes (a Governor since 1901 and Chairman from 1921 until his death in 1950).

G. H. Norris, a Governor and Old Boy gave £1,000. Before building commenced it was decided on the advice of the architects, by now Spalding and Theakston, to raise the whole structure by 2 feet; this, at a cost of £500, would make the buildings more impressive when viewed from the railway, and also improve the drainage system. The Foundation Stone was laid on 4th April 1914 by Mr. W. B. Hodgkinson, J.P., the Chairman of the Governors of the Ephraim Hallam Charity. The ceremony was followed by lunch at the Town Hall.

It had been a close-run thing. During 1912, when numbers had reached 172, it was decided that entry would have to be restricted for the next year, as 'the Board of Education has commented adversely on the size of several of our classes and has refused to countenance it'. Numbers did indeed fall to 166 in 1913; but the Board's reactions to the 185 in the School in December 1914, and the 192 a year later, are not recorded. Meanwhile Mr. Samuel Kay had bought the Greek Street site for £5,000; the buildings were used thereafter as a Central School, and Evening School, and a hall for hire. In 1923 the site was cleared and presented to the town for the erection of a War Memorial and Art Gallery, which stands there today.

The move to Buxton Road took place during the Christmas holiday of 1915. Classes were held there from 20th January 1916, and the formal opening ceremony was performed on Saturday, 29th January, by Colonel George Dixon, Chairman of the Cheshire County Council. A guard of honour was formed by the School detachment of the Stockport Battalion of the Cheshire Volunteer Regiment. The Colonel inspected the guard and then received from the architects a gold key inscribed 'Stockport Grammar School, 1487'; with this he unlocked the west door and declared the buildings open. In spite of the difficulties of the War the contractors, Daniel Eadie and Son, had taken only a little over twenty months to complete the work on schedule.

The West front of the School in 1916.

The new buildings were designed for 250 pupils in ten classrooms grouped in a two-storey block on one side of the quadrangle; next to this, forming another side, was the Hall, named after Ephraim Hallam; other benefactors were commemorated in the Sykes Lecture Room and the Norris Gymnasium. Strangely, the Founder was not to be remembered until 1979, when the Headmaster's residence was named Shaa House.

The number of boys quickly exceeded 250 – by the end of the year there were 256; by the end of the decade, 324. Naturally, more staff were required, and many of those appointed by Daniels were destined to spend the rest of their teaching careers at the School: W. Potts taught Art from 1915 to 1948; L. S. Goddard, Mathematics, 1916–62; L. Griffith, General Subjects, 1916–37; E. H. W. Conway, Classics, 1918–48; H. D. Smith, Mathematics, 1919–63; B. Varley, Geography, 1919–50; W. A. Paine, French, 1920–52; T. J. Anderson, Physical Education, 1921–42; A. Johnston, History, 1925–68; A. T. Boak, Physics, 1927–54. W. Sidebotham had already taught Music since 1888 and S. Balston, French and German since 1897, both Pemberton appointments. A. South, Chemistry, 1905–37, and J. L. Taylor, Woodwork, 1906–34 were Daniels men from Greek Street. The contribution of these men to the success of the School in its new home was immense. If it can be claimed that the young men who spend a short time in a school before moving on provide the vitality, it is equally true that those who devote their whole lives to a single school give the continuity, tradition, and wisdom which are equally, if not more, important.

The Great War also caused the appointment, for the first time because of the absence of men in the Forces, of lady teachers to the staff. In keeping with the times the ladies were strictly segregated and used the rooms on each side of the front door. In spite of the segregation however, one of the ladies, Miss Blackledge, did later on become Mrs. Daniels. The Headmaster himself was an aloof and somewhat austere figure in public, betraying his emotions only twice – when he announced, on the afternoon of 11th November 1918 to the assembled school, the signing of the Armistice, and when some sixth-formers presented him with a gift to mark his marriage. He was lost for words at the time, and had to apologise and thank the donors later in private.

The ending of the War was marked first of all by an extra week's holiday, but plans were in hand for a more permanent reminder of the 'war to end all wars'. One hundred and sixty Old Boys – a very substantial proportion – had volunteered before conscription was introduced, and many more thereafter, and the names of the fifty-two who did not return were to be recorded on the School's War Memorial. Spalding and Theakston designed this to fit in the Hallam Hall, the work was executed by Mr. J. L. Taylor, then woodwork master at the School, and the Old Boys' Association paid for it. The Memorial was unveiled by the new Chairman of Governors, Colonel Sir Alan Sykes, on 11th November 1921.

The Hallam Hall in 1916.

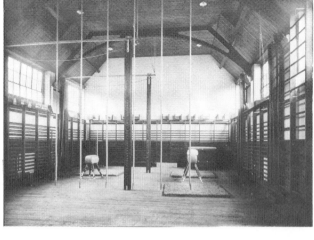

The Norris Gymnasium (now the Geography Room) in 1916.

The Sykes Lecture Theatre in 1916.

The Quadrangle in 1916.

With peace had come the School's first Sixth Form as that term is understood today, with nine members. There were three full subjects for the new Higher School Certificate – Pure Mathematics, Applied Mathematics, and Physics. Apart from the practical work in Physics, Daniels himself taught the whole course. In addition, there was subsidiary English. Two of the boys from amongst these pioneers went on to study Mathematics at Cambridge, with great success, to Daniels' pride: J. G. Adshead of Caius College, who eventually became Professor of Mathematics at Dalhousie University, Nova Scotia, and W. L. Edge of Trinity College, who held a similar post in the University of Edinburgh. Both were holders of the John Benjamin Smith Exhibition from School, and both won other Exhibitions and Scholarships during their Cambridge careers. When Edge graduated he was one of the two Smith's prizemen in his year.

The 1920s were years of consolidation, following the upheavals of war, removal, and expansion. The field at Adswood was sold, and new playing fields were laid out at the front of the School, facing the railway line. These were formally opened by the Mayor, Alderman Charles Royle, in September 1923. In 1924 it was decided to publish annually a Yearbook as a prospectus, and this continued until paper rationing caused its abandonment during the Second World War. The House system – with stunning lack of originality called North, South, East, and West – was introduced for Games and athletics.

During the Great War Daniels had proposed that the Headmaster should retire on his sixtieth birthday (and his assistants on their 50th!), and with this in mind he tendered his resignation in July 1928: he would be sixty in December. The tributes paid to him on his retirement were warm and heartfelt. The Governors recorded their thanks at their meeting on the last day of 1928. During his Headmastership of twenty-five years, the number of boys had increased from 90 to over 300. The move from Greek Street – where at one stage he had had 60 boys being taught in the old Headmaster's house – to Buxton Road had gone smoothly, and Daniel's most illustrious pupil, Edge, had just become a Fellow of Trinity College, Cambridge. At the public ceremonies, the head boy, David Blank (later to become a Governor), presented Daniels with an inscribed gold watch; from the staff there was a standard lamp, a set of fish knives and forks from Sergeant, a pen from the Debating and Literary Society and the Cercle Français.[2]

Building work at 4, Chestergate, in 1921 revealed parts of the Schoolhouse wall, partly of wattle and daub and partly of 2½" brick (therefore before 1625, when the size of brick was standardised at the modern 3"). Also uncovered were some floorboards, one of which is pictured here, together with a small pocket knife and two marbles – an Elizabethan schoolboy's?

Staff v Boys Tennis – 1923.

65

The Sixth Form in 1923.
[Reproduced by permission of Mr. H. D. Smith.]

The Greek Street School in May 1921, shortly before the site was cleared to make way for the War Memorial and Art Gallery which stands there today. Following on the move to the new School at Buxton Road in 1916, the Greek Street building was bought by Mr. Samuel Kay for £5,000, and used thereafter as a Central School, an Evening School, and as a hall for hire.

Skipton Girls' High Sch.
Form VI.A.
Brennand, Marjorie
Lawson, Winifred
Peaton, Annie
Rushton, Edith
Smeall, Elizabeth M.
Stirk, Mary
Taylor, Margaret
Wood, Margaret B.

Sleaford Kesteven and Sleaford High Sch. for Girls.
Form VI.
Harpham, Mary A.

Southport Clarendon Sch.
Form VI.
Bowker, Dorothy M.
Leighton, Ruth M. J.

Southport High Sch. for Girls.
Form Sen. VI.
4,10,11 Clark, Dorothy E.
Elliott, Jean
13 Heyes, Edith M.
Hopson, Marjorie
Whiteley, Miriam de B. R.

Southport King George V. Sch.
Hardie, William H.
Johnston, William S.
Long, George E.
Ratledge, Ernest D.
4 Smith, Sydney H.

Form VI. Sc.
Fincken, Christopher W.
Marshall, Joseph E.
Shatter, Gershon
Smith, William H.

Sowerby Bridge Sec. Sch.
Form VI.
Bywater, Dorothy
Cawood, Mary
Crawshaw, Mary
Crowther, Albert
Farrar, Elsie
Killin, Catharine
Longbottom, Phyllis
Mallinson, Ada
Mallinson, Ralph
Sharp, Alice M.

Stafford Girls' High Sch.
Form U. VI.
Marden, Alice M.
Percival, Edna E.
Rowland, Elsie S.
Tubb, Lilian E.

Staveley Netherthorpe Gr. Sch.
Form U. VI.
Finch, Emily

Form VI. U. Sc.
Ashley, George L.
Beeley, John W.
Davies, Ronald A.
Haywood, Stanley
Hopkinson, Kenneth
Jackson, Charles L.
Madin, Alfred B.
Roe, Wilmot J.
Woodcraft, William L.

Form VI. Sc.
Mellor, Sydney D.

Stockport Fylde Lodge High Sch.
Form VI.
5 Holland, Gladys

Stockport Gr. Sch.
Form VI.
Balston, John M.
10 Blank, David
Briggs, James H.
Garrett, Reginald
17 Lamont, Peter A.
Patten, Henry

Stockport High Sch. for Girls.
Form VI. U.
Fletcher, Helena H.
Henshaw, Joan
Hepplestone, Marian
Hope, Winifred M.
Nelstrop, Mary F.
Wharton, Margaret J.
Williams, Kathleen M.
Wrathmell, Margaret

Stockport Sec. Sch.
Form VI.
Critchlow, John

Stockton-on-Tees Gr. Sch.
Form VI.
Thompson, Norman

Stockton-on-Tees Sec. Sch. for Boys.
Form VI.
Briggs, George E.
Foster, Alan W.
Ingman, Arthur L.
Ross, Malcolm K.
13 Thompson, Ronald S.
Wilson, Arthur C.

Stockton-on-Tees Sec. Sch. for Girls.
Form VI.A.
Lodge, Eva

Stoke-on-Trent Hanley High Sch.
Form U. VI.
Brereton, Arthur R.
Bromley, Colin W.
Clay, Winifred R.
Hancock, Marjorie
Handley, Florence G.
Hawksworth, Emma
14,17,18 Kearton, Christopher F.
Light, Freda E.
Miles, Robert S.
17 Shaw, Thomas
10 Singer, Samuel
Smith, William
Sockett, George B.
21 Woodroffe, John H.

Stoke-on-Trent Longton High Sch.
Form U. VI.
Bagnall, Philip
Baker, Constance L.
Berkin, Albert J.
Cleaver, Lilian W.
Dodd, William
Durman, Olive
Fairs, Marionne
Fearn, Charles H.
Griffiths, Reginald J.
14,17,18 Hadley, William H.
Holmes, John L.
Jackson, Charles
Moffatt, John
Nixon, Ernest
Pedley, Nellie
Pitt, Norman
Saville, George
Tranter, Nelly

From the Joint Matriculation Board's List of successful candidates for the Higher School Certificate Examination in July 1928. From King George V School, Southport, both W. H. Hardie and W. S. Johnston went to Oxford and on to teach at Stockport Grammar School in 1934. From Stockport Grammar School, J. M. Balston was first editor of the Stopfordian and Stanworth Balston's son, and David Blank went on to become a Governor.

The War Memorial and Art Gallery.

GILKES[1]

The new Headmaster was Mr. Christopher Herman Gilkes, an Oxford graduate and for the previous six years a Housemaster at Uppingham. He lost no time in stamping his mark on the School: in his first report to the Governors he noted that

'The curriculum has been completely revised and especially in English has been brought up to date. Life-saving classes have been started. A very successful expedition of 100 boys and twelve masters was organized to visit Port Sunlight: I hope that this will be the beginning of a series of semi-educational tours to factories.' [It was.] 'The drought had produced many weeds: but the use of detention boys and voluntary weeding have done much.'

Extra-curricular activities continued as before, probably the most memorable being the rambles in the Peak District organized by masters such as Mr. A. South and Mr. H. D. Smith.[2]

The School was inevitably to be affected during the 1930s by the Great Depression:[3] even the forces of Nature were conspirators:

'During the storm on Tuesday last' [reported the *Stockport Advertiser* on 1st August 1930] 'the pinnacle of the main gable on the south side over the Sykes lecture room was struck by lightning and split, some of the stonework being dislodged. Fortunately the holidays had begun and there was no-one about at the time. If the lightning had struck a foot nearer Buxton Road it would have gone right though the roof and considerable damage would have been done. As it was the damage was slight.'[4]

A payment of £12 9 8d was eventually received from the insurance company. There were some bright spots: Horace Lamb received a knighthood. Curricular novelties continued: the Headmaster, himself a Classicist, reported on Speech Day:

'we have made the experiment of allowing boys in the 5th to choose their own work for two hours a week, with the interesting result that a dozen boys have chosen to do Greek.'

There was also what was to become a recurrent feature of Gilkes's reports – as indeed it had been for a half a century already – regret at the parents' lack of faith or courage, which resulted in boys leaving early and not going on to University. 1931 saw the first Old Stopfordians' Annual Dinner actually to be held in School (the Associa-

tion had been renamed, reviving one of the old forms of the name of the town, in 1927). The School Magazine, *The Stopfordian*, soon celebrated its fifth birthday, thereby enduring longer than its predecessor, which had lasted only from 1898 to 1902. The Dramatic Society founded in 1930 and the School Orchestra (1931) went from strength to strength, with public performances the success of which invited favourable comparisons with professional groups.

During 1934 the Music master, Mr. William Sidebotham, retired after 46 years' service. His connection with the School went back even further, for he had himself been a pupil, first entering in 1870 when Hamilton was Headmaster. His musical talents had not been confined to the School, for he had been first a choirboy at St. Matthew's in Edgeley, and then organist for the Sunday afternoon services at Barnes' Convalescent Home in Cheadle, followed by eight years as organist at St. John's, Heaton Mersey, then 20 years at St. Peter's, Stockport, and finally 34 years at the Parish Church, St. Mary's, from which he finally retired in 1944.

Another master who retired in 1934 was Mr. Stanworth Balston, who had taught French and German. He it was who inaugurated Continental excursions, for in 1925 he took a dozen boys to Bruges for eight days on an educational visit. His son John had been the first editor of *The Stopfordian* in 1929. Mr. J. L. Taylor, Woodwork master since 1906, also retired. He was responsible for the carving of the School's War Memorial, as well as for work in many local churches, and was also a first-class photographer.

The number of boys continued to grow, and by the mid-30s there were 380, in a building designed for 250. As the 450th Anniversary of the Founding of the School was approaching, and as the School had in 1933 achieved Public School status, with the admission of the Headmaster into the Headmasters' Conference, it was decided that it was an appropriate moment to extend the accommodation, with the building of two 'temporary' classrooms and a new Art Room. With this building and some rearrangement in existing rooms, the Science departments were allowed to expand, with Chemistry gaining half as much space again, and Physics three times the amount it had, by moving its laboratory into the old Art Room. These plans were duly put into effect, and the new building was ready for opening in good time for the celebrations.[5]

The end of the Summer Term in 1937 – 23rd, 24th, and 26th July – marked the culmination of the Anniversary. Proceedings began on Friday the 23rd with a Commemoration Service at St.

An aerial view of the School, taken in the early 1930s.

School Production 1933 – 'Captain Brassbound's Conversion'.

George's, Heaviley, attended by masters and boys, Governors, parents, and friends. The Chairman, Colonel Sir Alan Sykes, read the lesson, appropriately taken from the 44th chapter of Ecclesiasticus, 'Let us now praise famous men.' The Lord Bishop of Chester, the Right Rev. G. F. Fisher, gave an address on the place of religion in education. After the service the congregation went on to the School, where the new rooms were formally declared open by Major T. C. Toler, Chairman of the Cheshire County Council.

During the Friday evening a banquet was held in the Hallam Hall, at which the principal guest was Colonel Sir Crisp English, the Prime Warden of the Worshipful Company of Goldsmiths, whose presence marked the coming together again of the Company and its erstwhile School. The relationship was taken a stage further in the following year, when the Prime Warden accepted for himself and his successors the office of Patron of the School. At the banquet and on behalf of the Company, Sir Crisp presented to the School a silver cup and cover 'as a memento of this great occasion and an emblem of good luck in the future'. The silverware had been designed and made by Mr. George Hart, of Chipping Campden in Gloucestershire, a craftsman in precious metals, to whom the freedom of the Company had been awarded in recognition of his outstanding work as a craftsman.

The Toast to the Founder was fittingly proposed by the Regius Professor of Modern History at Oxford – Maurice Powicke, Old Stopfordian. He remarked that Sir Edmond Shaa

'was one of four people mentioned by Shakespeare who founded schools. He came in a very dignified society. Henry VI founded Eton, Cardinal Wolsey founded a School at Ipswich, Archbishop Chichele founded a school at Higham Ferrers as well as a College at Oxford, and Sir Edmond Shaa, Lord Mayor of London, founded the Stockport Grammar School.'[6]

Each guest was presented with a brochure, which recorded the story of the School, compiled by Mr. B. Varley and the forerunner of his History.

Saturday saw the annual Sports Day: no records were broken, except perhaps in the case of the rainfall. The weather cleared somewhat for Monday, however, and Speech Day was held as usual in the Quadrangle. The prizes were distributed by Sir Frank Fletcher, formerly Master of Charterhouse. The most popular announcement – from the boys' point of view at least – was that of an extra two days' holiday to mark the Anniversary.

To commemorate the event in more permanent fashion, the Old Stopfordians' Association presented one hundred guineas to buy an organ. Members of the Association also contributed as individuals – Mr. Thomas Hidderley added £100 and Mr. Henry Bell £250, and Mr. Peter Peirce undertook the cost of building a special gallery in the Hallam Hall. The inauguration ceremony took place in October, when the President of the Old Stopfordians, Mr. J. S. Southworth, presented the organ to the School. The initial recital was given by Mr. D. I. Steele, who later joined the Music staff of the School.

An instrument of smaller but yet great importance was the 'talkie cinema' acquired by the School at about the same time. The money to buy this was raised by various activities organized by Mr. Arthur South, Second Master, who retired at the end of the year. Appointed originally as a Physicist in 1905, he had become the School's first 'Second Master' in 1918. Among his many activities he had founded School Lacrosse and arranged Sixth Form walks for many years; during the War he tended the School's allotments by the Fives Courts, before the playing fields were laid out. One master who did not live to see the Anniversary was Mr. Llewellyn Griffith, who had died suddenly in January. He had been at School for over 21 years, teaching general subjects.

After the exhilaration of the Anniversary came the grim reality of impending war: discussions took place with the Borough Surveyor and a Major Foster on Air Raid Precuations. It was found that everyone could fit into the cellars, if the need arose, but £200 had to be spent on fans to improve the ventilation. In lighter vein,

'The Governors could not recommend the change over to Rugby Football from Association, as the traditions of the School must be maintained.'

There was a minor flurry later in the year with the opening on 8th September 1938 of the new buildings for the Local Authority's own boys' grammar school. Once again the two schools became neighbours, for the Authority had chosen to build on the Mile End Hall estate, one of the sites considered by Dr. Rayner, the then Chairman, and his colleagues thirty years earlier. Almost until the day of opening the new buildings were unnamed, and most people probably thought that it would continue to be the 'Stockport Secondary School'. Instead it was named 'Stockport School', thus using one of the names which had been applied to Sir Edmond's Foundation, probably from its earliest days, though the first written reference dates only from 1597. The naming did not cause any lasting embarrassment to either side, and the same friendly rivalry and relationship between the two schools continues, it not being unknown for pupils at the one to go on to become members of staff at the other.

During 1939 the approach of war seemed inexorable. New electric lighting was installed in the cellars, soon to become the air-raid shelters. The war was eleven days old when School opened again, 'as usual', on Thursday, 14th September, the only concession to the new circumstances being a change in the hours: the morning sessions now ran from 8.50 am to 12.15 pm, the afternoon from 1.30 to 3.30. Everyone had to carry a gas-mask at all times, and an air-raid practice was held on that first afternoon. In time, it was to take only three minutes from 'alarm' to 'all in' – an impressive performance, especially with numbers exceeding 400 with the arrival of 'refugees' from William Hulme's Grammar School and the Manchester Grammar School.

Further changes owing to the war were introduced during May 1940: homework and Saturday morning school were cancelled, and Games were held on Friday afternoons. These changes proved to be only temporary, however, and life soon returned to normal. Masters began to be called up, and once again were replaced by lady teachers. The first Old Stopfordian fatality was reported – Private Peter Pratt of the Cheshire Regiment, one of many past pupils serving with that regiment; the Commanding Officer of the Sixth Battalion was another Old Stopfordian, Colonel Sidney Astle. Boys still at School responded readily to the call to assist in gathering the crops during the summer holiday 'harvest camps' held mainly in the Chelford and Congleton areas. The holidays were in

fact split up into two portions of three weeks and one week, with three weeks back at school in between. Other boys took up duties in the ARP, with many of the older ones gaining qualifications in the organization. Their training proved invaluable from September on, when air raids on the area began in earnest. Stockport itself was bombed first on the night of 2nd/3rd October, with four people killed in Portwood; pieces of shrapnel were recovered from the flat roof over the cloisters after the particularly busy night of 20th/21st October. Davenport Park was bombed on the night of 14th/15th November, but the School escaped again, though the nearby house of Mr. M. J. H. Cooke, Headmaster of Stockport School, was very badly damaged. The entrance to the School from Buxton Road had to be closed until the 19th while an unexploded bomb in Corbar Road was dealt with.

To save precious fuel, sheep were occasionally used on the front field instead of a motor-mower to keep the grass in check, though it probably did not matter too much, as for a short period the field could no longer be used anyway for Games, owing to the telegraph poles and other obstacles laid and dug there to thwart landings by German gliders and paratroopers. Despite the privations of wartime, the School prospered, with virtually all the societies and sports continuing with vigour, apart from lacrosse (where equipment was hard to obtain – as were 'Fives' balls). Decorations for bravery won by past pupils were announced at morning prayers, and invariably earned the boys a half-holiday.

The Headmaster and his Staff – 1938.

71

PHILPOT

During 1941 the Mastership of Dulwich College fell vacant and Gilkes, wishing naturally to return to his old school and occupy the place once held by his father, applied. He was successful, and tendered his resignation from Stockport with effect from 31st October. There were 173 applications for the now vacant post, and from a shortlist of eight Mr. Frederick Harold Philpot, a Housemaster at Cheltenham College since 1921, was chosen. He had been educated at Westminster Abbey Choir School, where he had been senior chorister at the time of the Coronation of King George V, and at Westminster School, whence he proceeded to St. John's College, Cambridge. He could not take up his duties until the following January, however, and Mr. W. A. Paine, Second Master since South's retirement in 1937, deputised.[1]

The wartime routine was enlivened by a series of afternoon musical concerts for secondary school pupils at the Davenport Theatre; by potato-picking at harvest time; by Christmas work at the General Post Office; by firewatching duties with the ARP, both at School and at Stockport High School (the latter venue being very popular, a girls' school and not to be confused with its short-lived 19th century boys' predecessor); and by the various fund-raising 'War Weeks': 'War Weapons Week' in 1941 raised £5,729; 'School Warships' in 1942 £5,900; 'Wings for Victory' in 1943 £10,571; 'Salute the Soldier' in 1944 £10,785; and 'Thanksgiving Week' in 1945 raised £14,100, and also won the boys an extra half-holiday.

In February 1942 Mr. T. J. Anderson, the Head of P.E., suddenly died. He had been an officer in the Great War, and joined the staff of the School in 1921. He had been called up briefly in 1940, and had not been returned to School for very long before his death, which came as a great shock. Later in the year the first of a series of athletic matches between School and Stockport School was held, organized by the respective P.E. masters (now Mr. W. D. Beckwith, an Old Stopfordian, from School and Mr. W. J. Colclough from Stockport School and later to be that school's historian). School was the victor by 105½ points to 68½. In the following year the contest was three-cornered, with engineering cadets from the Technical College joining in, but School was again victorious. Later in the year there was a special excursion by tram to Manchester Art Gallery to view the King's Stalingrad Sword of Honour. The sword was made by Mr. Leslie Durbin of the Arts and Crafts Exhibition Society and of the Red Rose Guild of Craftsmen. The visit originated at the request of Sir George Courthope, Prime Warden of the Goldsmiths' Company, who expressed to the Headmaster his wish that the boys should have the opportunity to see this fine example of the work of the Company. The boys were allowed into the Gallery before the public, and after they had seen the sword the Chief Accountant of the Company talked about the Sword and answered questions.

In 1944 the East Cheshire ATC sports were held at Stockport School, and here again the Grammar School contingent (550 Squadron) was victorious, though numerically one of the smallest. Appropriately the Director of the ATC, Air Marshal Sir Leslie Gossage, presented the prizes at Speech Day the following week. A new Junior School was opened on 8th June in a converted house – 'Listad' – in Davenport Park. This project was the first to be overseen by the new Clerk to the Governors, Mr. T. R. Ellis, an Old Stopfordian who had been appointed when the previous Clerk retired in 1942.

By the end of the war numbers had increased to 458, which included 60 in the recently re-housed Junior School, the success of which was indicated by the 136 candidates for the 28 vacancies at the previous Entrance Examination. Under the terms of the 1944 Education Act, the Governors opted for 'Direct Grant' status, whereby the School received a grant direct from the Government in return for offering a quarter of the places (either 'free' or assisted) for boys from the areas of adjacent Local Education Authorities. For those whose parents paid fees, a system of fee remission was in operation, whereby only those with income above a certain level paid the full amount. The Scheme was approved by the Ministry of Education early in 1946.

Meanwhile the School 'Sergeant' (in fact Lt. Col.!) R. Miller had decided to resign, because his father, who had in fact been carrying out the duties of Sergeant since his son had rejoined the army in 1941, was now too old and wished to retire. A temporary replacement was hastily found, but it was not until the end of 1946 that a permanent appointment was made, that of Sgt. P. Merrey, recently retired from the Derbyshire Constabulary.

On Sunday 10th November it fell once again to Sir Alan Sykes to unveil the War Memorial, now containing the sixty additional names of Old Stopfordians killed during the Second World War. A separate bronze plaque was dedicated to the memory of Flying Office Charles Hyde, RAFVR, the only member of staff killed during the war, who

School Squadron 550 of the ATC at its camp at Crosby on Eden – 1944.

The Headmaster and his Staff – 1947.

died in action over Germany in December 1944.

By the end of the year all the other masters who had been in the forces had returned, and life was beginning slowly to get back to normal. Money however was still scarce and the introduction of Biology into the curriculum, first discussed in 1946, was deferred indefinitely. Two innovations during 1947 proved to be popular, and became annual events. On 20th March there took place the first Founder's Day Service at St. Mary's Church. Here Sir Edmond's parents had been buried, and here the School had probably had its first home. A kinsman of Sir Edmond, Sir John Kenward Shaw, of Eltham, was Guest of Honour and addressed the congregation. Since the 1949 service, when Latin was heard in the Church for probably the first time since the Reformation, the Founder's Psalm (no. 130) has been chanted:

'De profundis clamavi ad te, Domine:
Domine, exaudi vocem meam.
Fiant aures tuae intendentes
in vocem deprecationis meae.
Si iniquitates observaveris, Domine:
Domine, quis sustinebit?
Quia apud te propitiatio est;
et propter legem tuam sustinui te, Domine.
Sustinuit anima mea in verbo eius;
speravit anima mea in Domino.
A custodia matutina usque ad noctem,
speret Israel in Domino.
Quia apud Dominum misericordia,
et copiosa apud eum redemptio.
Et ipse redimet Israel
ex omnibus iniquitatibus eius.'[2]

On 15th December 1947, to replace the School Concert, the first Carol Service was held in St. George's Church, Heaviley. Like the Founder's Day Service, this too has developed into an impressive annual event.

During 1948 two long-serving members of staff retired. Mr. E. H. W. Conway, the assistant Classics master, had to resign through ill-health. Though only 53, he had been associated with the School for 44 years, having been a pupil at Greek Street, and had been in charge of Greek since 1938. The other master leaving was Mr. Walter Potts, the Art master, who, during his 33 years of service, had seen the arrival of every other current member of staff. Several of his paintings still hang at School.

The great success of the Junior School prompted the Governors to set up a Preparatory Department so that boys could be admitted at the age of 5. This in its turn was so successful that, within four months of its introduction in 1949, the available places for the next four years had been booked, so

that no new applications could be considered for admissions before 1953! 1949 also saw the introduction of Rugby football in place of Association, 'to make better use of the space', a decision then and since deplored and regretted by the Old Stopfordians' Football Club. With a 'new' sport came new names for the Houses. North became Nicholson, named after the earliest known pupil, William Nicholson of Reddish, later Headmaster, who died in 1597. South became Arden, after John Arden of Underbank Hall, who left School for St. John's College, Cambridge, on 25th March 1728. For East the new name was Warren, named after the Lords of the Manor from the 13th to the 19th centuries. And West House became Vernon: Lady Vernon gave the land for the Greek Street School in 1829, and Lord Vernon endowed his Latin Prize in 1874.

Academically, 1949 was Philpot's best year so far, a fitting tribute to the new masters he had appointed and to those returned from the War. In his first Annual Report seven years earlier, he had mentioned that 16 boys had gained Higher School Certificates; this year the number was 41; and the following year no fewer than 18 Old Stopfordians obtained degrees at Cambridge alone.

On 21st May 1950 the Chairman of Governors died. Sir Alan Sykes had been Chairman since 1921, and a Governor since 1901 when his father had died. As early as 1923 he was noted as having 'more offices than he can remember', and the number increased as he grew older: his life was dominated by public service in the widest sense. If memorial were needed, the thriving School provided it. He was succeeded by Col. Geoffry Christie-Miller, and Mr. Frederick Towns became Vice-Chairman. A gift of £250 from Sir Alan's will went towards the making of tennis courts, and in due course a Trust Fund was established, of which the School has been a great beneficiary over the years.

A new organ was installed in the Hallam Hall during 1951 as a further War Memorial, and it was inaugurated with a series of recitals during the November of that year. The previous instrument, a small electric organ presented in 1937, was no longer adequate, but it had certainly proved its worth, when in 1946 W. L. Wyatt, then head boy, in passing the examination for the Diploma for the Royal College of Organists, had achieved a Distinction, probably without precedent for a boy still at school. The new organ was built by Rushworth and Dreaper of Liverpool, to a design drawn up in consultation with Mr. D. I. Steele and Mr. G. C. Verney of the School's Music staff. The oak casework, grilles, and console screen were executed to the design of the organ-builders by Mr.

NICHOLSON HOUSE

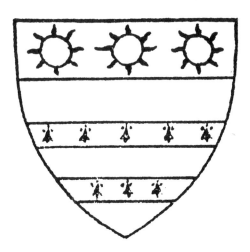

WARREN HOUSE

Tenebo

ARDEN HOUSE

Patientia Vinces

VERNON HOUSE

Ver Non Semper Viret

The House Shields.

Edwin Bromley, Handicraft master, and Mr. Ernest Abberley, of the School maintenance staff. With the installation of the new organ, the Headmaster took the opportunity to introduce monthly non-denominational services in the Hallam Hall, and these were to become a regular feature of School life for many years. It was in fact hoped eventually to build a new Hall to cater properly for the ever-expanding School, and to convert the Hallam Hall into a Chapel.

On 25th February 1952 Mr. W. A. Paine, Second Master since 1937, suffered a heart attack and died. He had been Head of Modern Languages since 1920, and was due to retire in five months' time. He had served with distinction in the Great War and had been awarded the MC; his lessons were marked by great thoroughness, and he was an early pioneer of audio-visual and Direct Method techniques of teaching French. He was Housemaster of Arden, and though forbidden by an old war wound from taking too boisterous a part in the sporting events of the House, yet he followed their activities closely and gave appropriate advice and encouragement. By a sad coincidence Miss E. M. Ridge of the Junior School died on the same day whilst posting a letter on Woodsmoor Lane.

Mr. A. T. Boak, Head of Physics, was appointed to succeed Paine as Second Master. Within months, however, he was taken seriously ill and was compelled to retire two years later. He had been at the School since 1927, and was the driving force behind the Natural History Society. In retirement he showed new skills as the owner of a sweets and tobacco shop in Kirkby Lonsdale. He died in January 1981.

Paine's successor was originally to have been Mr. W. H. Hardie, who had joined the staff in 1934. Immensely popular with both Masters and boys, he was a tireless worker in almost every School activity. But it seems that during his war service in Egypt and Italy he contracted tuberculosis. Although he returned to the School staff after the war, he was later compelled to spend some time in a sanatorium. He then came home, but was not allowed back to School for another year. He caught a bad cold and, thinking that the disease had returned, took his life. The news of his tragic death stunned everyone. He had been Form Master of 3A, and they wept at the announcement in Assembly next morning. He was only 42.

In spring 1952, the BBC broadcast, as part of radio series, a dramatised account of the School's history. The narrator was Professor F. C. Williams, an Old Stopfordian then at Manchester University and the inventor of the 'Manchester Automatic Sequence-Controlled Calculating Machine' (widely and more succinctly known as the 'Electronic Brain') – the first computer in the world with its own memory. Other radio presentations included one of the monthly services in 1954, and the School Choir in 1955. The demand for places continued to grow: in 1952 there were 200 applicants for the 29 Senior places, 55 for the 10 in the Junior School; in the following year 310 for 44 Senior places (every so often, three forms were admitted instead of the usual two), 70 for the 10 Junior. The 1952 'A' Levels resulted in five State Scholarships, two Stockport Major Scholarships, two Stockport Major Exhibitions, and three Cheshire Major University Scholarships – a record up to that time.

But School life was not narrowly academic: excursions had featured since the days of Gilkes and the 1929 visit to Port Sunlight. There was now a regular visit abroad for skiing; organized by the master in charge of German, Mr. Wolfgang Herman, the first had taken place in 1947, the year

after his arrival at Stockport. The Art Master, Mr. J. T. Stanley, had led archaeological digs to Bakewell for the Sixth Form and organized his first foreign visit to the Pyrenees. Mr. F. J. Norris took a party to Paris; Mr. D. J. Roberts, recently appointed Classics Master (and one of the wartime evacuees from the Manchester Grammar School) was taking boys sailing on the Norfolk Broads; and Mr. J. G. Gosling with the Venturers, and Mr. Theodore Horn with the Railway Society, were also travelling far and wide.

More space was needed to keep up the increase in numbers. In 1952 at the Chairman's request, the Stockport Playing Fields Society leased nine acres of land off Castle Farm Lane to the School for 99 years at an annual rent of thirty shillings. This was soon augmented by a further three acres immediately adjacent, donated to the Old Stopfordians' Association by the Vice-Chairman (in memory of his brother, Mr. Harry Towns) and Mr. Thomas Harrison (in memory of his son Peter, killed during the war). The Headmaster's house in Davenport Park was taken over completely by the Junior School, and a new one built for him – costing £4,621 5 10d! – during 1954. Plans drawn up by Mr. Gilbert Bullimore were soon unveiled for a new Science Block, to be built by the side of the tennis courts. Local businesses responded generously to an appeal from School, and a generous grant was received from a fund which had been set

5.0 p.m. CHILDREN'S HOUR
Other Children's Schools
2—Stockport Grammar School
Programme arranged and written by Bertha Lonsdale

Presented by F. H. Philpot, Headmaster

and a former pupil, F. C. Williams, O.B.E., F.R.S.
Professor of Electrical Engineering, Manchester University

Historical research by Benjamin Varley
(formerly Geography master)

Produced by Trevor Hill

5.50 ————434 m.————

From the Radio Times for Sunday 27th April 1952
[Reproduced by permission of the Editor of Radio Times.]

up by leading industrialists to help Independent Schools to provide buildings and equipment for Scientific teaching and research. The Block, built by J. J. Oakes & Son, was duly opened on Speech Day, 17th July 1957, appropriately by Professor Williams, who had recently become the first recipient of the Benjamin Franklin Medal of the Royal Society of Arts, 'to individuals who have attained early distinction, with promise of future achievements, in the promotion of arts, manufacture, and commerce'.

The detailed planning for the equipping and use of the new Block was in the hands of the newly-appointed Head of Physics, Mr. J. H. Avery. Up to this time all the Science teaching had taken place in the top corridor overlooking the tennis courts; here were the Sykes Lecture Room, a small Chemistry preparation room, a large Chemistry laboratory, a small Physics laboratory (which had been the Art Room prior to the 1937

expansion), and a small room in the tower. The Physics department moved out completely to the new building and Chemistry – abhorring a vacuum – expanded to take over the space vacated. The opportunity was now taken, having been so long postponed, to introduce Biology into the curriculum. Here the advice of Mr. Arthur Ellis, Head of Science at Cheadle Hulme School, was to prove invaluable, there being no experience of the subject at Stockport. As if to celebrate the opening of the new Block, the following year saw the record total of 23 State and Local University Entrance Awards, together with three Open Awards and four other places at Oxbridge: this from a Sixth Form of only 80 was no mean achievement. An average of 75% of leavers was now proceeding to University.

In February 1958 Mr. Benjamin Varley died. Born and bred in Stockport, he had identified himself with the life of the town and the School. He

Professor F. C. Williams opens the new Science Block on 17th July 1957, watched by Colonel Sir Geoffry Christie-Miller (Chairman of Governors), Mr. F. H. Philpot (Headmaster) and Alderman F. Cross, the Mayor.

had been Head of Geography from 1919 until his retirement in 1953, and later became a Governor, representing the staff of the School. His greatest memorial was the History of the School, but by the terms of his Will he also bequeathed money to endow two prizes, the Hulsean Divinity Prize and the Benjamin Varley Geography prize.[3]

During 1959 Mr. Theodore Horn, head of Classics, retired. He had first come to the School in 1921, leaving in 1931 to become Headmaster of North Manchester High School, and then returned in 1941. He took an active part in many School societies, and was also an editor for the Oxford University Press and official of the Assistant Masters' Association. In retirement he visited many places in the Classical World, edited selections from Xenophon's *Hellenica*, and wrote a pamphlet, *The School in the Sixties* to supplement Varley's History. He died in December 1969.

By 1960 there were 454 in the Senior School (including 105 in the Sixth Form), and 158 in the Junior School; applications for the 29 Senior places exceeded 300. Academic excellence was matched with extra-curricular activities of every description – from drama through sport to foreign travel. Together with Headmaster Philpot in the Senior School and Mr. R. D. H. Reeman, an Old Stopfordian, Master in charge of the Junior, only 33 members of staff were employed, carrying a heavy load but seemingly willing and certainly able to perform almost miracles.

Changes were at hand, however. The Headmaster had decided that he would retire when he had completed 21 years at the School; the Chairman of Governors had recently celebrated his 80th birthday, and was considering his future commitments; the Bursar had also decided to retire: it seemed that there would be a new team at the top to take the School on from its 475th birthday. The Anniversary was marked by a luncheon given in the Hallam Hall on 18th July 1962, presided over by the new Chairman, Lt. Col. J. A. Christie-Miller, Sir Geoffry's son. He spoke of the Founder, and looked forward to the future:

'With the ability to adapt itself to the changing requirements of the times, the school still lives, and its reputation stands as high as ever among the inhabitants of Stockport and the surrounding districts, and in educational circles beyond the extended parish of Stockport.'

In his farewell remarks at Speech Day, the Headmaster confined himself to the past 25 years, comparing 1937 – when there were six Old Stopfordians at Oxford and two at Cambridge – with the present, when there were 22 and 15 respectively. Five past pupils had this year obtained first-class Honours degrees, an achievement performed only once before, in 1950.

Tributes were paid to Mr. G. C. Verney, 'our Director of Music for almost 20 years, who has raised our music . . . to the very high standard achieved by the School today. Those who have attended our carol services and Founder's Day services, also our concerts and Sunday afternoon choral services, will agree that we owe a tremendous debt of gratitude to Mr. Verney'. Mr. L. S. Goddard, the Bursar, had also retired. Originally

The 1962 Pavilion, designed by Mr. Gilbert Bullimore (as had been the Science Block). The clock was a personal gift from Mr. Bullimore.

appointed in 1916 to teach Mathematics, he had soon revealed himself as an organiser 'par excellence'. Before long he became part-time Bursar, and on his retirement from teaching in the late 1950s he had taken on the post full-time.

Philpot's retirement brought to a close an era in the life of the School. He had successfully led the School from the dark days of war, through a time of austerity thereafter, and on to the easier but still challenging years of the 1950s. The tribute of Mr. W. S. Johnston, Second Master since 1954, on Philpot's retirement, cannot be bettered:

'The Staff found him always kindly and considerate. He listened to complaints, resolved disagreements on the rare occasions when they arose, encouraged the young and humoured the old – all this with unruffled composure. Boys proved him just and understanding. He took an interest in most School activities, and there are few societies and clubs which he did not help by his advice and encouragement. With parents Mr. Philpot shewed his genius for tact and diplomacy. Irate fathers departed as meekly as doves; tearful mothers raised a smile as they left the building.'

Mr. and Mrs. Philpot retired to Solva in Pembrokeshire, and in time he became an Independent member of Haverfordwest RDC, and Chairman of the Parish Council. Clearly Stockport's loss of this calm, civilised, distinguished man was Pembroke's gain.

F. H. Philpot, M.A., Headmaster 1941–1962.

Speech Day was held in the Quadrangle (weather permitting) until the move to the Davenport Cinema in July 1962. Here Mr. Philpot gives his Headmaster's Report in 1961.

SCOTT

The new Headmaster was Mr. Francis Willoughby Scott, MA, educated at Hymers College, Hull, and St. Catharine's College, Cambridge, where he was an Open Exhibitioner. During the war he had served in the United Kingdom, India, and Ceylon, and retired from the army as a major in the Royal Artillery. Between 1947 and 1953 he was Head of History at Plymouth College, and in 1950 he was awarded a Page Scholarship to travel in the United States. Prior to his coming to Stockport he was Headmaster of Batley Grammar School, in Yorkshire.

Scott's first year as Headmaster was to prove rather quiet (in comparison with what was to come later), though not totally without incident. On the academic side, General Studies was introduced to the Sixth Form 'A' Level curriculum, and the School bade farewell to Mr. H. D. Smith, whose career had begun in 1919 under Daniels. He was to teach Sixth Form Mathematics with great distinction from 1921 until his own retirement. He had been Housemaster since the 1920s of then East, now Warren; officer commanding the ATC from 1944 until 1955; tennis-player, golfer, and wicket-keeper; and a hiker of some distinction.

A sad loss during 1963 was that of a most distinguished Old Stopfordian, Professor Sir Maurice Powicke. His academic career culminated in his appointment as Regius Professor of Modern History at Oxford in 1928, a position he held until 1947. Knighted in 1946, he continued to live in Oxford, to study in a room provided by his old college, and to write – in particular his volume on the Thirteenth Century in the Oxford History of England. He was a Governor during the 1920s, and President of the Old Stopfordians during their 50th Anniversary year.

1964 marked the fiftieth anniversary of the laying of the Foundation Stone of the main building, and soon parts of the School came to resemble a building site yet again. Work had already commenced on the front terrace, with the erection of new rooms (for the Lower Sixth) on each side of the front door, and the fives courts were about to be demolished. These latter had to go to provide matching bricks for the new rooms and the space needed for the next stage in the expansion, a new Gymnasium beside the 1962 Pavilion. In a series of meetings with parents, the Headmaster with the new Bursar, Wing Commander J. M. Gilchrist, outlined the visions of an enlarged future: the new Gymnasium would release the old one to serve as a temporary library; and then the building of a new hall, with some additional rooms, would allow the library to move to the Hallam Hall. The old Gymnasium could then become additional space for Art, while Geography took over the old Library. An appeal was launched to raise the necessary funds, which it was envisaged would total £100,000.

£30,000 had been raised by the end of the year. There were other gifts, too: new oak doors, given by Sir Geoffry Christie-Miller, adorned the side entrance; cathode-ray oscilloscopes had been donated by Ferranti Ltd. and Professor Williams (who had recently received the Hughes medal of the Royal Society); £1,000 had come from the Sir Alan Sykes Trust towards the cost of the Sixth Form rooms; and Mr. Charles Royle, MP and Old Stopfordian, and Mr. David Blank, Old Stopfordian and a recently co-opted Governor, were arranging to provide £100 to endow a Sixth Form Essay Prize in memory of the former's father, a Governor from January 1923 until his death the previous November.

The retirement of Sergeant Merrey marked the end of another era – not only the departure of a friend and character, but the last of a long line of School Sergeants going back to the appointment of Sgt. Sash in 1888. Though Sergeant was no longer in charge of 'drill' (that task now falling to the PE Department), he still had plenty to do, receiving visitors to the School, answering the telephone, issuing stationery, working the duplicating machine, looking after the dinner register, the absentee book, the late book, distributing correspondence, and looking after casualties. One duty only was not passed on – for it was decided to convert the bell system from manual to electrical operation.

The lack of a comprehensive and up-to-date register of Old Stopfordians had always been keenly felt, and the work of compiling it was entrusted to a small body of Sixth Formers, marshalled by two prefects, E. J. Thomas and T. Volk. The work involved in compiling the Register – in particular tracking down current addresses – led directly to a Grand Reunion of past pupils and staff, which took place on Saturday 26th June. Typical summer weather marred and eventually curtailed the outdoor events, but in spite of this the day was a great success, with more than 800 attending. Building on the goodwill thus created Mr. Goddard, now retired to Buckinghamshire, set about contacting every Old Stopfordian living within a reasonable distance of London, and on 6th November the inaugural meeting and Dinner of the London Branch of the Association took place,

The Headmaster and his Staff – 1963.

with the Headmaster and Mr. Hitchcock, the President, travelling from Stockport to attend.

The election in October 1964 of a Labour Government committed to the concept of 'comprehensive' education seemed to threaten the School's Direct Grant status. As a result of the 11+ examination, each year fifteen scholars came from Stockport and fifteen from Cheshire (which included Bramhall and Hazel Grove), so between a half and a third of the intake paid no fees, and the rest benefited from a remission scale for those of limited means. The Governors declared their willingness to be flexible and co-operative with the Government's ideas, but pointed out that, while the School was probably already comprehensive as regarded area and by virtue of its covering a fair cross-section of the population, it could not contribute to the particular concept (by accepting the full range of abilities) without destroying itself. The Government set up a Public Schools Commission to investigate the Direct Grant Schools: this brought together the sixty Heads of Direct Grant schools in the Headmasters' Conference in much the same way as the Taunton Commission had led to the creation of the Conference itself in 1869.

The Commission's Report was finally published in March 1970. It is worthwhile to anticipate events a little and quote at length from the Governors' Statement of that same month:

'We hope to see evolution rather than revolution in the educational field. We know that the School is not large enough to become a comprehensive unit itself, and even if it were large enough, we would not wish to change its character completely in that way. We wish to continue as a Direct Grant school in friendly co-operation with the local authorities, and we are prepared to be flexible in any new arrangements that we may be able to make together, but we feel that we must preserve the quality, traditions, and record of this School and keep faith with the benefactions of the past and present. We would therefore favour complete independence rather than full integration as a "sub-unit" into the comprehensive system. We would regret having to choose complete independence, because it would mean that boys of ability from poorer homes could not afford to enter the School. We believe that the record of Direct Grant schools justifies confidence in the system – the aim should surely be to bring more independent schools (boarding and day) into the Direct Grant scheme.'

If the School's size had made it too small to be a 'full comprehensive unit', it also caused problems in that a two-form entry of 60 boys meant that some Sixth Form courses could not be economically viable. The Headmaster urged that the inter-

Sgt. Merrey retired in 1964 – the last in a line of School Sergeants dating back to the appointment of Sgt. Sash in 1888. [Reproduced by permission of the Stockport Express Advertiser.]

mittent admission of an extra form should be made regular to provide a three-form entry each year. But it was not simply a matter of taking one extra form: as the increase progressed up the School, it would become the equivalent in time of five extra forms, and it would not be until 1971 that such an expansion could be accommodated, as the building programme came to fruition.

Building in fact continued unabated. The Fives Courts had fallen and the Gymnasium had risen, to the design of Dex Harrison, who had inserted the new Sixth Form Rooms into the front of the School. The Gymnasium was opened in a simple ceremony on 26th May 1966 by Alderman Sir Wesley Emberton, Chairman of the Cheshire County Council. During the following Summer holidays the Dining Hall was doubled in size by the addition of a prefabricated section, and shortly afterwards the kitchens were also enlarged.

The Fives Courts 1916–1965.

More important than any political uncertainty during the 1960s was the vast expansion of Higher Education, with new universities, polytechnics, and colleges, together with the recognition of the need for 'A' levels to enter them, the Services, and the professions. No longer did a sixth former of limited means need to win a scholarship to go on to higher education: admission secured a grant from the Local Authority. All this meant that for the first time all pupils were aiming for 'A' levels, and could be helped and encouraged by discussing careers and progress with their masters and parents. Behind the scenes 1962 saw the reorganisation of university applications through a central clearing house – UCCA – and this required a confidential report of each candidate. It had been the custom since Gilkes's day for masters to meet monthly to discuss the boys' progress, and now a simple record card contained all the necessary information, supplemented from time to time as necessary, and formed the basis of this report.

While internal forces were causing the expansion of the School, external forces were once again working to contract it. One of the proposals to relieve traffic congestion on Buxton Road seemed to envisage – details were difficult to obtain – using the trackbed of the railway line together with a 100 feet wide portion of the field to create an urban motorway. This threat to make 'a small school' even smaller exercised many minds during 1967, and it was only the building of a new block at Stepping Hill Hospital – next to the railway line and across one of the proposed carriageways – which finally scotched the plan.

Following the completion of the Gymnasium, the next major step in the building programme was a Hall, with Harrison as architect again. Two sites were considered for this, one on the cloister side of the Quadrangle, the other spanning the Drive. The former was never seriously in the running, for it would have involved the demolition of the caretaker's house and garage, removed the First Forms' playground and provided no new classrooms: indeed, if built, it would have rendered the 1937 extension itself too dark for further use. The Appeal Fund had now reached £65,000, of which £23,000 had been spent on the Gymnasium; it was decided to continue the Appeal for a Hall costing in the region of £90,000. The Foundation Stone was duly laid by Alderman W. C. Knight, Mayor of Stockport and Old Stopfordian, after the Founder's Day service on 20th March 1969.

Sadly, this ceremony was destined to be the last visit to School by Sir Geoffry Christie-Miller, who died suddenly a fortnight later whilst on a cruise to the West Indies. His loss was felt sharply, not only at School, but also in the town, and many tributes

An aerial view of the School – 1965.
[Reproduced by permission of Airviews (Manchester) Ltd.]

were paid to his work and a lifetime given to public service. There were a few areas of life where he had not been involved – his interests ranged from Stockport Infirmary to the Territorial Army, Stockport Lads' Club to the Boy Scouts, the Trustee Savings Bank to the NSPCC. He had been a Borough Councillor and Magistrate, a Director of Swain & Co. and Christy & Co., and a Liveryman of both the Fishmongers' and Felt-makers' Companies in London. In the midst of all these, School had had the benefit of his being a Governor for 46 years (he was first nominated by the Borough Council in 1923) and Chairman for eleven. He continued as a Governor after the Chairmanship had passed to his son, Lt. Col. J. A. Christie-Miller, who guided and inspired the expansion of the 1960s and 1970s.

The first casualty in building the Hall was Room 5, form room for many years of Mr. A. Johnston, who retired in July 1968, having been Head of History since 1925. There is a touch of the actor in every good schoolmaster, but it must be doubted if there was ever a man in whom the two professions were so evenly balanced. The thoroughness which marked his teaching was matched only by that which he and his wife Eleanor showed in preparing the School Plays. And not only those plays, be it noted. One year the then *Manchester Guardian* published a list of the ten best plays from Dramatic Societies in the area. The ten were chosen from more than 260, and of those ten, four had been produced by the Johnstons – one at School, one by the Johnston Company, one at Altrincham Garrick, and one at Adswood Community Centre. She had been Form Mistress of Junior C from 1950 to 1962 and taught with patience, sympathy, and understanding, introducing many boys not only to drama (as was to be expected) but also to cricket and football. He was Form Master of the Literary Sixth for many years, and Housemaster of the present Vernon, then West, since 1931. An avid traveller in Mediterranean lands and an early exponent of the use of audio-visual teaching aids (using lantern slides in a lecture in 1929), he was the only man to have led his bride from Church under an archway of History notebooks suddenly held aloft by two lines of boys from School. It was typical that on his retirement he and his wife moved – not to somewhere in England, but to the South of France. Typical it was too that when a car became a necessity, he took and passed (first time, of course) the French driving test.

By the end of the 1960s an old School tradition – lessons on Saturday morning – had been abolished. Wednesday afternoon games had been absorbed into a five-day teaching week, with School matches, music, and other activities

F. W. Scott, M.A., Headmaster 1962–1979, with some long-serving colleagues. At rear, W. S. Johnston (Second Master) 1934–1975, J. G. Gosling 1945–1980; centre, F. J. Norris, 1934–1975, Mrs. E. Johnston 1950–1962, T. Horn 1921–1931 and 1941–1959; front, H. D. Smith 1919–1963, A. Johnston 1925–68, Mr. Scott, W. D. Beckwith (O.S. 1915–1924) 1942–1970.

(including detention) on Saturday morning.[1]

In May 1970, to further the Appeal, the School was privileged to hold a Reception at the Gold-smiths' Hall in London for Old Stopfordians and their ladies. The Prime Warden, Sir Alan Wilson, a Past Warden, Sir Owen Wansborough-Jones, and the Clerk, Mr. W. A. Prideaux, represented the Company at the occasion, while the Chairman of Governors and Mrs. Christie-Miller and the Head-master and Mrs. Scott welcomed the guests. Some of the Old Stopfordians present, including Lord Royle (since 1964 the first Stopfordian Life Peer), had attended the School at Greek Street. The Reception was a great success, and strengthened still further the link between the School and the Company.

At the end of the Summer Term Mr. W. D. Beckwith retired. His career at the School had started at Greek Street as a boy in 1915 and continued until 1924; he had returned as a master in 1942 to teach PE and Mathematics in the Senior School, and Nature Study in the Junior School.

Soon he had added Music, Physics, and Chemistry to his repertoire, together with the ATC and House Boxing.

The Conservative Election victory in 1970 had removed, for the time being at least, the prospect of the School's being compelled to join the Independent sector, and allowed thought to be given at some length as to what Independence might entail. It was quickly realised that a new building to house the Junior School – which was desirable in any case – would be vital if Independence were to come. Plans were commissioned, and it was hoped to commence building in June 1973 and have the work finished within a year.

A second Grand Reunion was held on 3rd July 1971, and this time the weather was glorious. Mr. Philpot travelled from Pembrokeshire for a gathering which was not primarily a fund-raising event, but rather a celebration of the building carried out over the previous fifteen years to provide extensions of both premises and facilities. There were numerous exhibitions, with Cricket and Tennis Matches between pupils present and past in which the honours were evenly shared. In the evening there was a Barbecue, with a Steel Band providing the music and All Star Wrestlers other entertainment. This was to be Philpot's last visit to the School: on 9th December 1974 he went for a drive near Haverfordwest, and died peacefully in his parked car. Strangely, Gilkes, his predecessor, had died in the same manner, in the same area, in September, 20 years previously.

Mr. J. G. Gosling and 1st XII Lacrosse – 1965.

Mr. J. H. Avery and 1st VI Tennis – 1965.

Mr. F. J. Norris and 1st XV Rugby – 1963

The Headmaster and his Prefects – 1967.

85

The Foundation Stone for the new Hall was laid on Founder's Day 1969 by Alderman W. C. Knight, Mayor of Stockport and Old Stopfordian.

Younger members of staff before the retirement dinner to Mr. W. D. Beckwith – 1970.

550 Squadron ATC at their Easter 1970 camp at R.A.F. Scampton, near Lincoln. In July of that year walkers from the Squadron set a new record of 18 hours 41 minutes for a 100-mile march, beating the previous record by over 4 hours! Sadly, the Squadron was disbanded at Christmas 1979, after being in existence almost 40 years.

Viscount Amory opens the new Hall – Founder's Day, 1972.

July 1971 also marked the retirement of Mr. W. E. Abberley, who had been head of the School's maintenance and ground staff since 1944. He had not only maintained the buildings, he had enhanced them too, with examples of his craftsmanship, such as the panels in the Hall and the Headmaster's Table, based on an original in Tideswell Church.

A new edition of the School Register was published at the end of the year, once again prepared by two prefects, this time M. R. J. Bestley and R. Hamilton.

On Founder's Day in 1972 the Prime Warden of the Goldsmiths' Company, the Viscount Amory, and the Clerk to the Company, Mr. W. A. Prideaux, journeyed from London to open the new Hall, and afterwards inspected the new buildings and met masters and boys. The only surviving pieces of the Greek Street building, the Foundation Stone and the Goldsmiths' Crest, now renovated by courtesy of the Company, were preserved under the arch. To commemorate the visit, the Prime Warden the next year, Mr. John Prideaux (whose father had been Clerk at the time of the 450th Anniversary), called at the School in April

with designs of a second cup and cover, which was commissioned by the Company from Miss Jocelyn Burton and was presented to the Chairman and Headmaster in July 1974.

In September 1972 the Vice-Chairman of Governors died. Mr. Frederick Towns had attended the School between 1898 and 1903. He had become a successful Solicitor, and had joined the Board as a representative of the Old Stopfordians in 1949. He became Vice-Chairman in 1950 when Sir Geoffry Christie-Miller vacated that position to become Chairman. Mr. J. C. Moult now became Vice-Chairman, and Mr. W. A. Kershaw was elected as one of the Old Stopfordians' nominees on the Governing body.

University awards at Oxbridge in 1973 equalled the 1954 record, with five Scholarships and Exhibitions. A half-holiday was granted in celebration: a reminder of the days when Pemberton granted half-holidays to celebrate his birthday. Meanwhile, two long-serving members of staff had retired. Mr. D. I. Steele, in charge of Music, had joined the staff in 1946, and over the years had instilled his own love of music into hundreds of pupils by means which, if slightly idiosyncratic, were enormously successful, and had nurtured talents as diverse as members of symphony orchestras and pop groups, and soloists. He inspired the memorable Christmas Carol Services in St. George's, Heaviley, and a collection of his compositions was recently published to commemorate his 75th birthday.

The cup and cover presented by the Goldsmiths' Company in 1974.
[Reproduced by permission of the Editor of Cheshire Life.]

Even longer-serving was Mr. Edwin Bromley, who had arrived in 1934 as a member of both the teaching staff and the maintenance department. He was an outstanding craftsman in wood, and the panelling for the organ and the Headmaster's Chair are just two examples of his work. He founded the Arts and Crafts Society, and outside the School was probably best-remembered for his Christmas-time collections (started during the war) of books and toys for the Infirmary. He commanded the ATC for some years, and was associated with soccer and later rugby and also cricket. Sadly, he enjoyed less than a year of his retirement before he died in February 1973.

July of that year saw the retirement of Miss Joan Thornely, who had first joined the staff in 1941, when there were only two Junior Forms (J.A. and J.B.), which occupied the two classrooms of the 1937 extension. She soon found herself refereeing football and umpiring cricket, and over the years became a well-loved and respected member of the staff. She provided the boys with a thorough grounding in the basic subjects of English and Arithmetic, and showed them how to help others less fortunate, with gifts to an Anglican Mission School in Lesotho and the RSPCA.

Mrs. Nellie Hawksworth retired in December 1974 after 24 years' service, first with her husband as joint resident caretaker and after his death as the catering manageress. She and her staff organized not only school lunches, but refreshments for all games and meetings, sports days, Speech Days, and Dinners and Lunches for the Old Stopfordians and several outside groups.

The high rate of inflation in the 1970s was threatening the building of a new Junior School, and a Sports Pavilion at the Dialstone Lane field. The Old Stopfordians' Association had been trying for many years to raise sufficient money to build the Pavilion, and indeed had sold the Harrison-Towns field some three years previously for this very reason. With great regret they decided to abandon the project in view of the ever-increasing cost. There was still the problem of ground security – large open spaces tend to attract trespassers, both harmless and harmful – and a bungalow was built, by the Sir Alan Sykes Trust, for a soon-to-be-resident groundsman. It was not easy to postpone building a new Junior School, but the cost of a conventional building was by now well into six figures and still rising. Meanwhile one of the adjacent houses on Clifton Park Road had come on to the market and School had bought it.

The plan which the Governors had in mind –which was carried out with great success – was to demolish this house, build the first phase of the new Junior School where the house had stood, and finally to demolish the then Junior School and replace it with the second phase, using Kencast prefabricated buildings. Everything went remarkably smoothly, and the new buildings were finally declared open on 2nd September 1975 by Lt. Col. Christie-Miller.

This was the Colonel's first appearance as an 'ordinary' Governor again. He had not been well early in the previous year, and decided to resign as Chairman, though he did remain on the Board for five more years as the Goldsmiths' nominee. His record of service to the community was very similar to his father's, but he had also been Deputy Lieutenant of Cheshire since 1963, and more recently High Sheriff of the county. He had been Master of the Worshipful Company of Feltmakers in 1956/7 (the tenth member of the family to hold this position), and president of the European Association of Hat Manufacturers between 1957 and 1964. He had been President of Stockport Historical Society since 1964 and a founder-member of Stockport Civic Society. He and his wife (a niece of Sir Alan Sykes) retired to the Cotswolds for a well-deserved rest from public service, though they remained as trustees of the Sir Alan Sykes Trust, a charitable fund established in 1954 and the main beneficiary of which has been the School. The new Chairman was Mr. J. C. Moult, with Mr. David Blank as Vice-Chairman.

The end of the Summer Term saw the retirements of two long-serving members of staff. Mr. D. B. Cassie, the Head of Chemistry, left after 27 years in the School, having started with a department which comprised one laboratory and half a lecture room (shared with Physics). As well as teaching his subject, he coached badminton, ran the Photographic Society, sang bass in the School Choir, refereed lacrosse, and acted as Careers Master for the Scientists. In his 'spare' time he sang in two other choirs, enjoyed Scottish Country Dancing, and walked.

Mr. F. J. Norris, the Head of Modern Languages, had first come to the School, on teaching practice, in 1933, and returned in January 1934 as Form Master of Junior A. He soon moved up into the Senior School. During the war he served in the Royal Corps of Signals and attained the rank of Captain. He returned to the School in December 1945 and was appointed Head of Department in 1952 on the death of Mr. Paine, with whom he had pioneered oral methods of teaching French back in the 1930s. Outside the classroom he ran the Debating and Literary Society and the Cercle Français, became Housemaster of Nicholson, and arranged lunch sittings, the prizes for Speech Day, and the purchase of text books and stationery. He had organized the School's first language laboratory in the mid 1960s, assisted in the Bursar's office, and yet still found time to engage in research into Victor Hugo's correspondence, which he pursued further in retirement.

At Christmas another master who had first arrived in the 1930s retired. Mr. W. S. Johnston, the Second Master and Head of English, had been appointed to the staff in 1934, initially as Form Master of Junior B. By 1937 he too had moved up to the Senior School. After wartime service in the RAF he had come back to the School, and with his friends Mr. Norris and Mr. Hardie had helped to introduce Rugby to the School. Since 1954 he had been Second Master, filling this difficult position with meticulous efficiency and good humour, qualities which also marked his teaching. His ability to organise often went unseen – though never unappreciated – since everything was done so unobtrusively and apparently without effort. He guided boys' applications to university, and numbered among his other activities the Housemastership of Arden, the Debating and Literary Society, and the Library. His commitment to School was matched by his commitment to his wife, whom he nursed through a long illness without ever missing a day at School. He died in October 1982.

In July 1976 Mr. J. H. Avery, the Head of Physics, retired. Having finished planning the new School Science Block, he proceeded to become more widely known in the world of Physics teaching. Both syllabuses and examinations were being brought up to date, and he was in the forefront of the new developments. As there was no suitable textbook, he and another schoolmaster in Rugby decided to write not one, but two, and he also wrote *The Mathematics of Physics* for Biologists, who often find the mathematical aspects of Physics rather difficult. He was a member of several committees and panels of the Joint Matriculation Board, and ran School tennis. He constructed the timetable, possibly the task which in any school calls for the supreme diplomat. Retirement did not bring rest, however, but an appointment to the Governing Body as the nominee of the Teaching Staff.

Meanwhile the return of a Labour Government in 1974 had once again brought into question the status of Direct Grant schools, and it was announced in Parliament on 11th March that it was intended to phase out the system over a period of seven years, commencing in September 1976. The implication of this was that Senior School fees – then £369 a year – would have to rise to at least

£550 for new boys. The possible impact on the School soon became apparent. The Entrance Examination produced the usual number of candidates (about 350), but of these half would be interested only if a bursary or some other sort of aided place could be provided. The response of the Governors was swift: they announced on 14th March 1975 that the School would go 'Independent' and they launched The Stopfordian Trust to provide the sort of bursaries which would be required. Response to the appeal was swift too, and by the end of the year more than £13,000 had been raised. This source of bursaries was soon augmented by a fund established by the Greater Manchester Council, and also in due course by the Government's own Assisted Places scheme, set up in 1981.

Momentum was maintained by the founding of a formal Parents' Association early in 1977. Parents had, inevitably in a Direct Grant school, always been closely involved since they were, numerically, the biggest source of income for new building projects, which could not be financed from fees; but the only formal organization had been the Ladies' Committee, in whose capable hands the Autumn Fairs and Scandinavian Evenings had prospered over the years.

At this difficult moment the Bursar fell ill. Wing Commander J. M. Gilchrist had been appointed Bursar and Clerk to the Governors in 1962, and to him had fallen the task – in addition to his ordinary duties – of arranging the financing of the numerous building programmes. Mr. J. S. Southworth, a Governor and Old Stopfordian, and for many years the School's represenative on the Stockport Education Committee, filled the breach during the Bursar's illness, and continued to do so after the latter's untimely death on 28th October.

The deaths had also recently occurred of Mrs. R. B. Heathcote, a Governor from 1949 to 1974,

who left a legacy of £500 to the School, with instructions to spend the annual income from this on books for the Library, and of Professor Sir Frederick Williams, Old Stopfordian. His invention of the first computer in the world to possess a memory has already been mentioned, but his work also included radar during the War and new types of electric motor later. He too had been a Governor, representing Manchester University between 1955 and 1969, and had been knighted in 1976.

The new Bursar and Clerk, Wing Commander V. A. Hodgkinson, took up his duties on 15th February 1978. If he had hoped for a gentle introduction to the life of the School, he was soon to be disappointed, for 1978 was to be the year in which far-reaching changes were to be set in motion. The major problem continued to be space – or to be correct, the lack of it! The School, now 600 strong with a regular three-form entry into the Senior department, was desperately cramped, despite Scott's building programme. The Old Stopfordians' Association had decided to use some of the proceeds from its sale of the Harrison-Towns field to build squash-courts, and the Parents' Association was about to launch an Appeal to raise money for a swimming pool, the lack of which had been bemoaned since the move to Buxton Road. The difficulty was that any additional building – of squash-courts, swimming pool, or even classrooms – could by now only take place at the expense of valuable playing-field space.

From his office window, the Bursar could see a quarter of an acre of dense undergrowth lying behind the School Pavilion; it was once the site of the Convent greenhouses and allotments, but now unused and neglected. An idea began to form in his mind, but the Governors were apprehensive about taking on more commitments – faced with the abolition of the Direct Grant, they had decided to go 'Independent', and in the circumstances they thought it best to consolidate and take stock, rather than expand. There the matter might have rested, but Hodgkinson had to meet Sister Elizabeth, the Headmistress of the Convent High School, to discuss the shared use of the sports facilities. He learned that that school would shortly be closing: the Roman Catholic Diocese of Shrewsbury, as the body responsible for its denominational education in Stockport, planned to build a new comprehensive secondary school in Cheadle, St. James's, and to convert St. Michael's on Nangreave Road into a Sixth Form College. The Convent High School thus had no independent future, and indeed discussions had already taken

Mr. C. R. Dalton and 1st XV Rugby – 1974.

place with the Local Authority for the possible redevelopment of the site.

Matters now moved quickly. At their next meeting on 2nd May, the Governors decided to approach the Provincial Headquarters of the Sisters of the Holy Family, the owners of the Convent, with a view to buying land for squash-courts. At this critical moment the Chairman of Governors suddenly died while gardening. Mr. J. C. Moult had attended the School between 1928 and 1934, and had maintained his connection thereafter through the Old Stopfordians' Association. He became Clerk to the Governors after Ellis's death in 1957, a Governor in 1962 when Gilchrist was appointed Bursar and Clerk, Vice-Chairman in 1973, and Chairman on the retire-ment of Lt. Col. Christie-Miller in 1975. His years as Chairman had not been easy – the abolition of the Direct Grant was a particular blow – but they were years of solid achievement. The Parents' Association came into being; the Stopfordian Trust was established; the School's financial arrangements were conducted on more commer-cial lines. He had especially in mind Sir Edmond's will and its provision

'to teche allman persons children and other that woll com to hym to lerne',

He had been a scholarship boy himself, and he wished to ensure as far as possible that families without financial resources should be enabled to send their boys to the School.

The Vice-Chairman, Mr. David Blank, who as School Captain had welcomed Gilkes to the School in 1929 and had seen the changes which followed, became Acting Chairman and Mr. W. A. Kershaw Vice-Chairman. The Governors urged that the purchase of the land should be pursued vigorously. During a visit by Hodgkinson to the Sisters' Provincial Headquarters in London, it became apparent that the whole of the Convent site – with its buildings – was on offer if requested. The strictest secrecy was maintained during the subse-quent discussions, for premature dis-closure of what was afoot was obviously undesir-able. Reports were commissioned from Surveyors and from the Fire Service: these confirmed that there should be no insuperable obstacle to the purchase. A price of £250,000 was agreed, and completion was set for August 1980.[2]

Having taken the plunge to buy the whole site, it was necessary to consider how best to use the new asset to the greatest benefit. It would have been possible simply to have overflowed into the addi-tional accommodation for, as we have seen, space

was already at a premium in the old premises. This option was never seriously considered, since the fees, already at £732 a year, would have had to rise by at least £100 simply to cover the increased running costs. The course the Governors decided upon was to increase numbers in planned stages to about 1,000, which would entail a much smaller rise in the fees, and also to admit girls: this would avoid any potential lowering of standards, for there was a demand for places for girls, and there was at least a moral commitment to take some of the Convent's Sixth Formers when it closed.

At the same time as the Convent negotiations were taking place, the Governors were also adver-tising for a new headmaster, for Mr. Scott had decided to retire at the end of the Easter Term in 1979. His period as Headmaster had been, to say the least, exciting. The 1960s were years of great opportunities and great expansion in education; in the 1970s the opportunities still existed, but the expansion was drawing to a close. This was the nature of the challenge to which he had had to rise. He rose, and surmounted it. Buildings are his monument – 'the Hall spans the Drive' – the tan-gible side; no less valuable is the spirit engendered by probably his greatest achievement – the Par-ents' Association, mentioned already. He would also be remembered for his visions of the future, even if these did not always command universal understanding. On his retirement he and Mrs. Scott – a source of strength and encouragement throughout the years in Stockport – moved to Plymouth, where they had long been accustomed to spend their summer holidays.

Other members of staff had retired the previous summer. Miss Seti Losli had been a part-time teacher of the violin since January 1947. By the nature of her rôle she was not known by very many of the boys, but those who did come into contact with her had no trouble in recognising both a

Mr. V. Wilcock and 1st XII Lacrosse – 1974.

Mr. H. D. Robinson re-founded the School Orchestra in 1963 and remained as conductor for 20 years, seeing it grow in strength and father several others over the years.

first-rate musician and a first-rate teacher. Mr. J. T. Stanley had been Head of Art since 1949, and as Form Master of 1A for most of those thirty years, was the introduction to School for almost half the annual intake. He introduced other things – the Marionette Theatre shortly after his arrival, the archaeological digs at Bakewell, First Form camps on Mull, hiking expeditions to the Lake District, the Dolomites, Venice, the Pyrenees, Spain, Greece, and – probably best known of all –Corsica, every Easter from 1960 to 1977. The first foreign visit had been to the Pyrenees in 1952 – a fortnight for £10: an age and a world away from today. Wanderlust affected him even in retirement, when he and his sister Phyllis deserted suburban Didsbury for rural Whaley

Bridge – nearer to walking country, of course, and to places he could paint. He became the first editor of the Parents' Association Newsletter, a valuable complement to the School Magazine.

An aerial view of the School taken in 1973.
[Reproduced by permission of Airviews (Manchester) Ltd.]

92

WRIGHT

From among the 130 candidates who had expressed an interest in the Headmastership, Mr. Hugh Raymond Wright was eventually chosen. It had been necessary to handle the appointment rather delicately, as when the post was originally advertised it had been for a boys' school, 600 strong; with the anticipated changes this would soon develop into a co-educational establishment of up to 1,000. Wright's arrival in April 1979 coincided with the announcement of the Convent purchase and the changes which would result. To meet the new challenge and greet the new headmaster, there was also a new Chairman of Governors: Blank had become temporary Chairman on Moult's death, and when he retired, the Governors elected Mr. W. A. Kershaw as Chairman. A successful businessman, he had been on the Board since 1972, and had been Secretary of the Old Stopfordians' Association between 1966 and 1970, and President in 1972/3. Mr. P. J. Rowlinson, appointed to the Board two years earlier in 1977, became Vice-Chairman. His experience in the building industry was to prove useful during the conversion and renovation of the Convent.

Wright had attended Kingswood School, Bath, whence he went as a Scholar to The Queen's College, Oxford, to read 'Greats' and to continue his interests in rugby and music. After teaching at Brentwood School in Essex, he moved to Cheltenham College, soon to become Head of Classics and afterwards housemaster. It will be recalled that Philpot, before his appointment to Stockport as Headmaster, had also been a master and housemaster at Cheltenham. The pace of change and innovation which the latter had initiated with his new Science Block in the 1950s, and which Scott had continued and quickened during his years, was now reaching its logical conclusion with the taking over of the Convent buildings and the admission of girls in September 1980.

Before that occurred, however, another old stalwart from the teaching staff retired. Mr. J. G. Gosling, Head of the Religious Education Department, had first been appointed in 1945 to teach PE. He had been taught how to play lacrosse as a boy at the Stockport Secondary School by the Physics master, Mr. William White, an Old Stopfordian, and after the war he reintroduced the game to the Grammar School. Of all the trophies which can be won in schoolboy lacrosse, only the Centurion Trophy, for under-13s, eluded his teams: but on 15th March 1980, in a match against William Hulme's School, the School under-13 team – the sixth such to have reached this final – was victorious by 8 goals to 5. He had also been Form Master of 1B for many years, providing a thorough grounding in Mathematics for many future Old Stopfordians, and had been an officer in the ATC. He had started the Venturers' Society in 1945, when he was asked by some boys to take them on a visit down a coal mine, and on Mr. Horn's retirement in 1959 had taken over the Railway Society too. In retirement he and his wife Olive moved to Bramhall, where he was kept busy by his continued involvement with another long established institution of the town, Stockport Sunday School.

In 1979 Mrs. Nancy O'Donnell also retired, having been for 23 years an indispensable part of School life – catering for numbers large or small, brewing tea and coffee, selling biscuits outside Room 18, applying plasters to wounded knees or offering sympathy to wounded spirits.

Early in 1980 a new Choral Society was founded, giving its first concert, Haydn's *Creation*, just three months later in St. George's Church, Heaviley. Work went on over the Summer Holiday of 1980 to ensure that the Convent buildings would be ready for the new term, when there would be girls in both the Sixth Form and the First Form. The record number of 650 – 375 boys and 275 girls – had taken the entrance examination in the previous March, and eight new members of staff had been appointed. An existing member of staff, Mrs. Sheila Renshaw, was ready to take up her duties as Senior Mistress.[1]

The novelty of girls on the premises was duly reported in the local press when term started, and quite quickly forgotten, too, as they settled in with very little fuss. The 22 girls in the Sixth Form quickly managed to produce a netball team, though it won only one of its six matches; the First Formers were much better, winning twelve of their twenty in netball, and four of their six in hockey. The Sixth Formers did however succeed in carrying the motion that 'The female species is superior' at the predominantly male Debating and Literary Society.

The new buildings on the Convent site were brought gradually into use over the next five years as the planned refurbishments were completed and the School slowly expanded with each new mixed intake. The opportunity was taken to provide the different subjects with their own suites of rooms making it possible for Departments to stamp their characters on their surroundings. The Junior School was expanding at the same time, with two forms (instead of one) at each of 7+ and 8+, with

H. R. Wright, M.A., Headmaster 1979–1985.

girls admitted here too for the first time. The new Squash Courts, named the Harrison-Towns Courts, were opened in 1981, in the presence of the sons of the original duo, specially invited for the occasion.

July 1981 witnessed the retirement of Mr. Wolfgang Herman, the Head of German since his appointment in 1946. He pioneered the use of television in his lessons, supplementing the film-strip projector and the tape recorder; out of School he pioneered postwar continental educational visits and, later, exchange visits with Ludwigsburg. As Secretary of the Manchester branch of the Association of Teachers of German, he had played a prominent rôle in attracting the Goethe Institute to Manchester. He had been for many years an Examiner with the Joint Matriculation Board, and latterly Chief Examiner for the Cambridge Board. And under his guidance countless little boys had learned how to set out their chess-men at the weekly meetings of the Chess Club. He died in March, 1986.

During the Autumn Term of 1981 a Memorial Service was held for Mr. A. Johnston, who had died on 22nd July. The Address was given by the Rev. Canon Peter Firth (now Bishop of Malmesbury), once an outstanding Boy David and Hamlet in School Plays. A Fund was launched at the Service to endow educational travel in the Mediterranean lands which Mr. Johnston had known and loved so well; over £3,000 was raised and the first recipient of the award was D. S. Hallas.

Peter Boardman, who had been at School between 1956 and 1969, was one of the best-known names in British mountaineering at this period. Though outwardly quiet and unassuming, he had a steely determination and a passion for mountains fired by his first visit to Corsica with Mr. Stanley's School party in 1964. After University he became National Officer of the British Mountaineering Council based in Manchester, and later Director of the International School of Mountaineering at Leysin in Switzerland. He was the youngest member of the British Everest expedition in 1974, reached the summit with Chris Bonington the next year, and with Joe Tasker climbed Changabang in 1978. This was the subject of his first book, 'The Shining Mountain'. He and Tasker were chosen by Bonington to be members of the 1982 British Everest Expedition, and shortly before he left Leysin he wrote for the Parents' Association Newsletter an account of his schooldays, affectionately remembered:

'Thanks to Mr. Durnall I see two automatic red ticks for a North sign (crossed) and a scale whenever I draw a sketch map, I cannot photograph an Himalayan paddy-field without looking for moving water, and whenever I see a settlement from the air I think "site factors".'

In January 1982 he came back to Stockport to speak of his mountaineering experiences; so many wanted to hear him that the venue had to be changed from School to the Town Hall. It was to be the last occasion on which many of his friends saw him, for he and Tasker did not return from that 1982 Expedition. They were killed – how is not known – on the night of 17th/18th May; it was impossible to find their bodies, and the climb was abandoned. Ironically, two great predecessors, Mallory and Irvine, died whilst attempting the same route in 1924. As a permanent tribute to Boardman and Tasker who died tragically young, School inaugurated a prize to encourage further works of mountain literature.

During early 1983 Mr. H. D. Robinson (who had originally joined the staff in 1952) was appointed to the new post of Proctor, two years after having laid down his baton as conductor of the School Orchestra since 1963. In the expanding School the administrative tasks were expanding too, and his appointment ensured the continued smooth run-

September 1980 – Girls!
[Reproduced by permission of the Editor of the Manchester Evening News.

ning of the dining room and assemblies, and the administration of 'O' and 'A' Levels. He also took over the editorship of *The Stopfordian* from Mr. D. J. Roberts, the Second Master since 1978, who had edited it from 1959.

The Headmaster of the Junior School, Mr. R. D. H. Reeman, celebrated 25 years as a Master during 1984, though his connection with the School went back to his years as a pupil between 1942 and 1953. He had overseen the steady expansion of the Junior Department, presiding over its growth and its tours of the site with equanimity, and its success with pride. He provided the link between the School and its past pupils, for he was the Membership Secretary of the Old Stopfordians' Association, no easy task, with members spread all over the world. Also celebrating during the year was Mr. J. M. Swallow, who had spent 21 years as Head of Mathematics. From 1971 to 1977 he had also been 'Head of Wasdale', a former one-roomed schoolhouse in the Lake District which he had transformed into the School's Outdoor Pursuits Centre, guided by seven years' experience on the Corsica trips between 1966 and 1972. His gentler indoor pursuits included the Choir, the

Bridge Club, the Change-Ringing Society, and School Tennis after Mr. Avery's retirement.

School Journeys had extended their scope with a lacrosse tour (with Williams Hulme's School) in 1982, music tours in 1979 and 1984 to the United States, and the first expedition (by minibus) to Morocco, also in 1982. Another first was the first Scholarship won by a Stockport Grammar School girl, Marie Calnan, to St. Peter's College, Oxford, in 1984. At Speech Day in that year the Headmaster was able to announce that from September the School would be fully co-educational, in fulfilment of the plan announced five years earlier.

The new school year saw the opening of a Language Centre, and the Adshead Computer Room, founded by means of a generous bequest from the will of Professor J. G. Adshead, who has been mentioned already in these pages and who had died in August 1979. Another Old Stopfordian in the news at the same time was Admiral Sir George Back: Stockport journalist Mr. J. D. Lovelock had travelled to Canada to visit some of the places associated with that intrepid explorer. Another past pupil, Dr. W. B. Whalley, had won the Back Award of the Royal Geographical

Society for his recent contributions to high-altitude research and the application of electron microscopy.

During 1985 Mr. A. P. Smith, the Head of German, celebrated 35 years at School. A tower of strength, he was for many years the Master in charge of the business side of the Library, supervising its odyssey around the School; he had helped with lacrosse, with the School's annual invasions of German-speaking Europe, with the financial side of the School Play. He sang in the Choir, and ran the Change-Ringing Society together with Mr. Swallow.

Numbers in the Senior School had by now reached 934 (576 boys and 358 girls) and in the Junior 258 (149 and 109). At this point the Headmaster resigned, to take up the Headmastership of Gresham's School at Holt in Norfolk. Wright had presided with calmness over six years of considerable outward change, while preserving the inner spirit of the School unaltered.

In July 1970 the Mayor of Stockport, Alderman J. E. Walton, unveiled a plaque which marked the Chestergate site of the School. At the extreme right is the Chairman of Governors, Lt. Col. J. A. Christie-Miller; next to him Alderman W. C. Knight, Governor and Old Stopfordian.

A second plaque, marking the Greek Street site of the School, was unveiled on Founder's Day in 1974 by the then Mayor, Councillor Mrs. Margaret Heys.

[Reproduced by permission of the Editor of the Stockport Express Advertiser.]

BIRD

D. R. J. Bird, M.A., Headmaster 1985–.

The new Headmaster was Mr. David Richard John Bird, MA, who had proceeded from St. Paul's School via the Royal Air Force to St. John's College, Cambridge, where he read Geography. A rugby blue, he had also played for the Barbarians. He had been a Housemaster at Cranleigh School, and then Headmaster of Dartford Grammar School in Kent for the eight years before his move to Stockport, and his arrival coincided with the departure of the record number of 69 entrants to University and 18 to Polytechnics and Colleges of Higher Education. With the expansion of the School, there were now three Carol Services: one for the Junior School at St. Saviour's, Great Moor, and two for the Senior, still at St. George's, Heaviley.

November 1985 saw the retirement of Mr. Joe Blackshaw, who had completed 20 years as Caretaker, having been the groundsman for the previous 20. He and his wife retired to Countess Street, in Heaviley, not far from the buildings and fields he had looked after for a lifetime so conscientiously, with cheerful whistle and every-ready smile.

During 1986 Mr. J. G. Durnall celebrated 25 years as Head of Geography. Building on the firm foundation laid years before by his illustrious predecessor Varley, he had ensured the continued high standing and success of the Department. He had overseen its expansion, and organized its field trips to many parts of the country. He was also Housemaster of Nicholson. And Mr. D. J. Roberts, the Second Master, was able to look back on his 35 years at School. Appointed Assistant Classicist to Horn in 1951, he had become Head of Department and Editor of *The Stopfordian* on the latter's retirement in 1959. He had been in charge of the Recorder Club; he had taken boys sailing at Toddbrook and Salcome; he taught so-called 'dead' languages but made them live: quieter and gentler pursuits than many, no doubt, but performed with enthusiasm and commitment. As second Master he had initiated two Headmasters into the ways of the School in his own inimitable style. In this task he was ably assisted by Mrs. Muriel Ellis, who had been the Headmaster's secretary since 1973.

Building work continued, with a second storey being added to the Junior School building to provide improved facilities for art, drama, and music; and the Orchard was brought, providing room for possible future development.

The School today is thriving academically, with staff who wish to teach, teaching pupils who wish to learn – an unbeatable combination; and thriving socially, with societies and clubs to cater for every conceivable interest. There are two orchestras, two bands, and three choirs. Drama has maintained its strong tradition, with a major performance each year. Computing is well estab-

The Senior and Under-16 Netball teams, 1985/6.

The Headmaster and his Staff – 1986.

lished, both in lessons and with a Club. Other clubs and societies include the Debating & Literary, Chess, Wargames, Photography, Science Projects, Mountaineering, Railways, and Venturers. School parties visit many different countries. The annual Industrial Conference provides valuable insights into the world of business, and the Community Service Programme helps the less fortunate members of society.

Sir Edmond's School is five hundred years old. We cannot know what the future will bring; nor did he. But in faith he founded his School, willing the means whereby others could emulate his success, and over the generations many have done so. In confidence now it enters its second half-millenium. The School has lived up to its motto:

VINCIT QVI PATITVR[1]

List of Schoolmasters:

1488	. . . . .
1496	Sir John Randall
by 1509	Sir Randall Hulton
17th September, 1521	Sir George Bamford
28th October, 1534	Sir William Chorleton
15th February, 1544	Scolemaister of Stopport (name unrecorded)
19th May, 1557	William Chorleton (reappointed)
12th June, 1559	Leonard Harrison
Christmas, 1564	Thomas Leigh, B.A.
29th March, 1565	John Brownswerd
21st May, 1565	Richard Heywood
1579	. . . Bamford
by 1587	Francis Lowe
by 1597	William Nicholson, M.A.
23rd January, 1598	William Lingard, M.A.
3rd April, 1601	. . . Kirke
25th September, 1601	. . . Lang
Michaelmas, 1601	. . . Nicholson
8th January, 1602	John Cobb, M.A.
7th August, 1604	Thomas Bower, B.A.
8th April, 1609	Luke Mason, B.A.
31st October, 1610	Walter Pott, B.A.
4th November, 1623	Thomas Rossen
8th June, 1625	Reginald Pott
7th February, 1628	Edmund Clough, B.A.
7th August, 1628	John Pollett, B.A.
9th November, 1630	William Plant
24th July, 1633	Samuel Edwards, M.A.
5th July, 1634	Bradley Hayhurst, B.A.
8th August, 1645	Randall Yarwood
17th September, 1647	Thomas Peirson
9th April, 1651	Rev. Thomas Coombes
1st July, 1668	Rev. Daniel Leech
28th September, 1669	Rev. Joseph Whittle, B.A.
6th March, 1674	Rev. Samuel Needham, B.A.
27th July, 1683	Rev. Timothy Dobson, M.A.
14th September, 1691	Rev. George Escolmbe, B.A.
20th January, 1693	Rev. William Dickens
1st December, 1703	Rev. Joseph Dale
20th February, 1752	Rev. William Jackson, M.A.
20th January, 1792	Rev. George Porter, M.A.
20th December, 1792	Rev. Elkanah Hoyle, M.A.
27th March, 1829	Rev. William Newstead, B.A.
10th January, 1832	Rev. Thomas Middleton, M.A.
29th July, 1847	Rev. William Gurney, M.A.
3rd September, 1860	Rev. Charles Gillingham Hamilton, M.A.
12th November, 1887	Rev. William Alfred Pemberton, M.A.
28th January, 1903	Alfred Edward Daniels, M.A.
1st January, 1929	Christopher Herman Gilkes, M.A.
26th October, 1941	Frederick Harold Philpot, M.A.
1st September, 1962	Francis Willoughby Scott, M.A.
26th April, 1979	Hugh Raymond Wright, M.A.
1st September, 1985	David Richard John Bird, M.A.

Over the west door of the School are four carved panels.

The first represents the founding of the School, showing Sir Edmond, a scribe, and some scholars; the arms of the Goldsmiths' Company are in the background. The inscription beneath reads 'Sir Edmond Shaa, Knight, Lord Mayor of London, a native of Stockport. He of his bounty provided this school. A.D. 1487.' [The date should be 1488, and to be strictly correct, Shaa should by styled 'Mayor'. The title 'Lord Mayor' was first used in 1486, two years after Shaa had held the office, and did not become general under 1534.]

The second shows Alexander Lowe making his will. The inscription reads 'Alexander Lowe, Mercer, Stockport, bequeathed his house and certain monies to this foundation. A.D. 1587.' [The date should be 1608.]

The third shows John Brogden laying the Foundation Stone at Greek Street; the inscription reads 'John Brogden, Esq., Prime Warden, laid the foundation stone of the school in Wellington Road South, September 8, 1830.' [The date is correct.]

The last panel shows a Speech Day: Governors sit behind a book-laden table whilst scholars receive books. The inscription reads 'Ephraim Hallam, Mayor of Stockport, 1860. By his bequest the Governors were enabled to erect this School 1915.' [The dates should be 1862 and 1914.]

101

The School Gates, provided in 1949 by the Hallam Trust.

The Gates, Drive, and 1972 Hall.

The front of the School.

The Doors presented by Sir Geoffry Christie-Miller in 1964.

The Dining Hall and the Junior School with its 1986 extension.

The Science Block.

Bell's House.

The Pavilion and Bell's House.

Appendix 1

EXTRACTS FROM SIR EDMOND'S WILL

"In the Name of God be it Amen, the xxthe day of the Monthe of Marche the yere of our Lorde after thaccompt of the Churche of Englond Mcccclxxxvijth and the iijde yere of the Reigne of King Henry the vijth, I, Edmond Shaa, Knyght, Cytezen and Goldsmyth and Alderman and late Mayer of the Citie of London, though I be visited with sikenesse of the visitacion of our Lorde Jhu Criste, Nevertheless being of hole mynde and in good memoir, not willing wt the helpe of God inasmouche as in me is to departe intestate out of this mortall life, make and ordeigne this my p'sent testament in the fourme that followeth."

Place of Burial.

"Furst, I bequethe and recomende my soule to my Lorde Jhus Criste, my Maker and Redemer, to the Most glorious Virgyn his Moder our Lady Saynt Mary, to the full glorious confessour Saint Dunstone and to the Holy Compagne of Heven; And my body to be buryed in the body of the Churche of Saint Thomas of Acres in London, that is to say, between the Pyler of the same Churche whereupon the image of Saint Mychell th'arch angell stondeth before the Auter there, callyd Saint Thomas' auter, and the nether ende of the same Churche . . . as nygh the same Pyler as my body there reasonably may be layde. And in consideracion that I have borne the office of Mayralte of the said Citee, I will for the honour of the same Citee that my body be brought from my house to the Parisshe Churche of Saynt Peterys in Chepe, where I am a Parysshen as the maner is, And from thens to my burying at Saint Thomas of Acres aforesaid in discrete and honest wise without pompe of the worlde."

Interment and Requiem.

"And I woll have xxiiij honest torches to be borne by xxiiij paide p'sons to convey my body from myn house to my said parisshe Churche. . . . And whereas thusage is in the Cite of London at burying of the body of a man that hath born th' office of Mayralte of the same Citee and at his Moneth mynde, for the Mayer, Aldermen, Recordour and other Worshipfull and honest Comoners of this Citee for to be p'sent in thair ppre p'sons: Therefor to thentent that they may understand that I was a trowe loving brother of therys and am in pfite Charite with them . . . , If it woll like the Mayer and his brothern the Aldermen and the Recorder of the Cite of London for to be at my

Dirige and Masse of Requiem . . . at my Monethes Mynde, I wolde tenderly desire them after the said Masse of Requiem . . . to take souche a repaste as myn executours by the sufferannce of our Lord God shall provyde for them."

(Then follow payments to be made to all officials and others present at his Mass; and a repast to be made for all of the Goldsmiths' craft in attendance. The funeral torches (i.e. large candles) are to be distributed to various churches in the city.)

Masses.

"Item, I desire the parson, preste and Clerks of the said Parisshe Churche of Saint Peters to do placebo, Dirige and Masse of Requiem devoutly . . . by the space of an hole moneth next suying after my discease. . . . Item, I bequeth to evry house of the iiij orders of Freers of the Citee of London xxs to . . . do a trentall of Masses for my soule in thair own Covent Churche."

Foundation of a Daily Service and Annual Obit at St. Peter's.

"I bequeath CCLI to be bestowed in bying or purchasing of lyvelode good and sufficiaunt by the discrecions of myn executours wt thadvice of Thomas Wode, Goldsmyth. And I woll that the same lyvelode be amortisyd and made suer according to the lawe to the person and Churchwardens of the Parisshe Churche of Saint Peter's in Chepe. . . . To this intent, that with the revenues comyng yerely . . . service shall dayly and ppetually be kept by rote in the said Parisshe Churche of Saint Peter's . . . forthwarde for evermore.

"Also . . . to have an honest obite yerely for evermore, . . . doing over eve placebo and Dirige . . . and on the morowe following Masse of Requiem for the soule of me, the said Edmond Shaa, and for the soule of Robt. Botteler, Goldsmyth, sometyme my Maister, and for the soule of the said Thomas Wode and for all crysten soules."

(Lengthy instructions concerning payment for all these services follow; also for bread, cheese and coals for the poor.)

Foundation of a Chapel and Obits at the Church of St. Thomas of Acre.

"Item, for asmoche as I have before assignyd my body to be buryed in the said Churche of Saint Thomas of Acres . . . I woll have an honest marble stone to be provydyd by myn executours after my discease for to be layde upon my sepultur there. And I woll also have ther made . . . at my cost and charge a convenable Auter for a Prest to sing thereat. And also a convenable closure of iron wele and workmanly wrought to close in the said Auter in maner of a Chapell. . . . And I woll have that closure to be made with a clenly dore of iron for to open and shette to, when nede shall require, and to stond lokkyd stille after that masse be doon. And I woll have a Prest to be founden at the cost and charge of the Maister and Brethrn of the saide place and of thair successours . . . for to syng his masse dayly for evermore at the said Auter . . . to pray spally for my soule and for the soule of Julyan my best beloved wife whanne god shall calle her unto his grace, the soules of my Fader and my Moder, my children, my brethren and sustren. And also for the soule of the moost excellent Prince King Edward the iiij, the soule of his noble suster late Duchesse of Excetre, the soule of late Lorde Herbert and for all the soules that I am bound to pray for, and for all cristen soules. . . ."

"Nevertheless, it is my will that if it fortune the said Maister and Brethrn or thayr successours any yere . . . to make default in the finding of the said Prestys, or that the same Prest cease of his singyng at the said Auter by an hole quarter of a yere togiders, they havyng no resonable cause of excuse . . . then I woll that the same lyvelode shall then remaign to the Wardens and Felliship of my said Craft of Goldsmythes of London. . . ."

The Foundation of the School and a Chapel at Woodhead.

"It is my will to have asmouche other Lyvelode to be prchaced by myn executors assone as they may goodly after my disease to me amorteysyd unto my felliship of the said craft of Goldsmythes of London in ppetuyte, yf they woll agree to have it, to thentent here under written, orels if they refuse so to have it, then to . . . som other honest crafte of this Citee, as by the discrecions of myn executours it shall seme best . . . to have an annuell and quyte rent of xvijli by the yere of lawfull money of Inglond, therewᵗ to supporte and susteign yerely for evermore the charges here under expressed. . . ."

"I woll that the wardens and felliship of the clothing of my craft . . . com in thair lyverey . . . to myn obite yerely for evermore. . . ."

(The Wardens are to hold a repast afterwards and gifts are to be made to poor men to pray for Sir Edmond's soul.)

"I woll that the said wardeyns for the time being have of the said annuell and quyte rent of xvij li yerely liijs. iiijd.

"With the residue of the said annuell and quyte rent of xvii li amountyng to xiiij li vi s. viij d, I woll

have two honest Preestes founded prpetually, ye oon of them to syng his masse and saye his other divine service in a Chapell that I have made in Longdendale in the Countie of Chestre. And pray sp'ally for my soule and for the soules of my fader and my moder and for all cristian soules. And I woll that he have for his salarye yerely for evermore of the said xiiij li vj s. viij d, residue of the said annuell and quyte rent of xvij li, the some of iiiij li vj s viij d.

Qualifications and Duties of the Schoolmaster.

"And I woll that the other honest Preest be a discrete man and connyng in Gramer, and be able of connyng to teche Grammer. And I woll that he sing his masse and say his other divyne s'vice in the Parisshe of Stopford, in the said Countie of Chestre, at souche an auter ther as can be thought convenient for hym. And to pray specially for my soule and the soules of my fader and moder. And I woll that the said connyng Preest kepe a gram scole contynually in the said Town of Stopforde as long as he shall contynewe there in the said s'vice, and that he frely wᵗout any wagis or salarye asking or taking of any person, except only my salarye hereunder specified, shall teche allman persons children and other that woll com to hym to lerne, as well of the said Towne of Stopforde as of other Townes thereabout, the science of grammer as ferre as lieth in hym for to do in to the tyme that they be convenably instruct in gramer by hym after their capaciteys that God woll geve them. And I woll that the same connyng Preest, withall his scolers with hym that he shall have for the tyme, shall two days in every weke as long as he shall abyde in that s'vice ther, that is to wite, Wedynysday and Fryday, come into the said Churche of Stopforde unto the grave ther wher the bodies of my Fader and Moder lyen buryed, and there say togiders the psalme of de profundis with the verscules and collette thereto accustomyd after Salisbury use, And pray sp'ally for my soule and for the soules of my Fader and Moder and for all cristen soules. And I woll that the same Preest teching Grammer there shall have for his salary yerely as long as he abyde in that s'vice there x li of the said xiiij li vj s viij d residue of the said annuell and quyte rent of xvij li. And for to corage my said Felliship the which woll agree to bere the charge of the said annuell and quyte rent of xvij li to be the better willed to the supportacions of the same charge for evermore, I woll that the same Felliship shall have for evermore the p'sentement, nominacion and admyssyon of the said two Prcestes of the said two s'vices and the removing and puttyng out of them and admyttyng of other into the same s'vice for causes resonable as often as the caase so shall require."

Public Works, Rebuilding the Cripplegate.

"Item, I bequethe to the making of high wayes lying about Horndon in the Countie of Essex . . . xxli. also of a soule high way lying . . . on this side Alvethlee in the same Countie xx li. It is my full wille that for as mouche as the Fellyship of my Crafte of Goldsmythes have made a certayn quantite or porcion of the wall of this Citee stonding on the west syde of the gate called Crepulgate, that therefor yf the Mayer, Aldermen and comennalte of this Cite can be contented and agreable . . . I woll that they (my executors) shall set up there a new substanciall and manly gate of stone to the honour of Almighty God and Worship of this Citee. And to the making of the same gate I bequeth cccc marcs. . . . In caase that the said mair, Aldermen and comon counsaill of this Citee woll geve thair assents there to . . . then I woll that myn executours do set up myn Armes and tharmys of the Felliship of my Crafte of Goldsmythes upon the said gate."

Restitution for Misdeeds.

"Whereas a kynnysman of myn called Rychard Shaa caused me xl winters passed and more to go wᵗ hym to a Mannys (man's) ground in the peke in Derbyshire to take a distresse there. And so we toke for a distresse there two oxen and drave them thense, the which I am suer cam never agayn to his possession that ought (owned) them. And because that dede was doon in my wanton dayes whanne I lakkyd discrescyon, therefor I have a remorce thereof now in these dayes being better advysyd. Wherefor I woll that myn executours . . . do enquire after that man that was so distraynyd in the Peke . . . or his kynnysfolke next of his blode. And if myn executours can finde any souche, than I woll that myn executours restore to that man . . . or kynnysfolke aforesaid xx s for the hurtes that he hath susteynyd" (Then follow directions for finding him) "And if none souche can be founde, thanne I woll that myn executours take good advise of som sadde Doctours of Dyvynyte to understand what is best to do wᵗ the said xx s for the wele of the soule of the said man that was distraynyd, and for the discharge of my conscience, And then myn executours to pfourme the same."

Charitable Bequests to 200 Poor People of Stockport and District.

"Item, I woll that my executours, assone as they may goodly after my discease, do bye asmouche walshe fryse half-white and half-blak or gray, and thereof do make at my coste CC party gownes: and

the CC party gownes and xijd in money with evry gowne, I woll be geven to CC poue persons dwelling in the Parisshe of Stopford in the Counte of Chester, whereat my fader and my moder lyen buried, and within the Parisshes of Chedyll and Mottram in the same Counte, and in the Parisshes of Manchester, Assheton, Oldon, and Sadylworth in the Counte of Lancaster, by the Counsaille and advices of the Curate of all the said Parisshes . . . to thentent that the poue persons there shuld have them which hadde moost nede unto them."

Gifts to Stockport and other Parish Churches.

"I bequeth to the Parisshe Churche of Stopford aforesaid as good a sute of vestements of blew velvet as by the wysdoms of myn executours may be bought wᵗ the some of xl mcs.

Item, I bequeth to the Parisshe Churche of Assheton aforesaid another sute of vestements blew velvet as good as by the discrecions of my said executours may be bought with a like some of xl mcs.

Item, I bequeth to be spent of my goodes upon the making of the Steple of the Parishe Churche of Mottrom . . . xl marcs."

Gifts to the Poor.

"Also I woll that myn executours . . . distribute among poure people at my moneths mynde . . . xx li . . .

Item, I bequeth to be destributyd . . . among poue housholders of the Warde of Crepulgate as well within as without in redy money v li.

Item, I bequeth . . . to the marriage of pouer maydens of good name . . . in the Citee of London, within xxiiij myles about the same Citee xx li."

(Also many other gifts, including distributions of 'brede among the poue prisoners of Newgate' and several other prisons.)

Gifts of Mourning Rings.

"I woll that myn executours . . . do make at my cost xvi rings of fyne gold to be graven with the well of pite, the welle of mercy and the welle of everlasting life . . . John Shaa and Rauf Lathum understonden right well the makyng of them. And the ringes I woll that myn executours distribute unto my lovers here ensuying, praying them tenderly to have my soule in thair good remembrannces."

(The sixteen persons included Dame Anne Browne, Dame Elizabeth Hille, Sister Cote, Sister Wode, Sister Kelk, Sister Harding and others. Other of the smaller beneficiaries were 'Ser John the Preest that useth to say Matens and Masse afore me' and 'Henry Harsnapp and to my suster his wife'.)

Family Legacies

"Item, I bequeth unto Julyan, my true, my mooste dyer, and my best belovyd wife mm li . . . she to have of the same some, part in redy money, part in plate. I bequethe to the same Julyan, my true wif, if she after my discease kepe her selfe a sole widowe and unmaryed during her life, all my stuff of householde, as well in the Citee of London as elles where wᵗin the Realme of England . . . all my plate and juely of Goldsmythes werk, and all my stuff and tools belonging to my shoppe and warehouse or werking houses of myn occupacion.

Item, I bequeth to Hugh Shaa, my welbelovyd soon, goddes blessing and myne, and in mony, plate and juely, the some of m li (£1,000).

Item, I bequethe to my right welbelovyd doughter, Kateryn Shaa, goddes blessing and myne and in mony, plate and juely, the som of m li."

Executors.

"I bequeth to my right especiall and tender loving freunde Ser Raynold Bray, knyght, to the intent that it woll like hym to take uppon hym the charge of the execucion of this my p'sent testament, and of my last Wille c li. And I tenderly desire the same Ser Raynold Bray for the tender zele that he at this time bereth, and at all times afore this of his great kindnesse hath born towardes me, that of the said c li it woll like him to bestowe xx mcks or xxv mcks uppon a goodly cuppe covered of silver and gilt, wᵗ som token to be made there uppon, that it cam from a Goldsmyth of his acquayntaunce, and to be occupied by him and my good lady his wife at souche seasons as may beste please them, to thentent that by the sight thereof it may cause them to have my soule the tenderlyer in thair remembraunces."

(Geoffrey Downes, Gentleman, obtained 50 marks; Thomas Rich, who had married Margaret, Sir Edmond's daughter, obtained £100 and John Shaa, Goldsmith, £100. Each was to have a cup made similar to that of Sir Raynold Bray.)

"And of this my p'sent testament I make and ordeign myn executours, my most dyer and my most best belovyd wife Julyan, my right especiall frend Ser Rainold Bray, Knyght, my Cosen Geffrey Downes, Gentleman, my son Thomas Riche, m'cer, and my cosen John Shaa, Goldsmyth, Citizens of London. In witnesse of all the prmisses to yis my p'snt testament, I have set my seale the day and yere aboverehercyd."

Appendix 2

RENT ROLL OF THE PROPERTIES CONSTITUTING THE SCHOOL ENDOWMENT IN 1496–7

Hereafter foloweth the yerely valure of all Sir Emonde Shaa landys and tenementys that he bequeythed by his Testament to the Wardeyns and to their successours to the performyng his last Will, whose names of tenauntes now dwellyng in the seyd tenementes atte fest of Cristmas the xiij yere of Kyng Henry the vijth, foloweth:—

Rentall

Faster Lane.

Mr Bartholomu Rede, for a grete mese	vjli xiijs iiijd.
Christofer Elyott, for a tenement	xls.
Thomas Baldok, for a tenement	xvjs.
John Mone, for a tenement	xiijs iiijd.
Summa	xli ijs viijd.

Bowe Lane.

Raffe London, for a grete mese	vjli xiijs iiijd.
Pers Barbour, for a tenement	xls.
Mathew Cardy, for a tenement	xxxiijs iiijd.
Summa	xli vjs viijd.

Watlyng Strete.

John Wilkynson, for a tenement	iiijli iiijs iiijd.
John Pooye, for a tenement	iiijli.
Robert Frende, skynner, for a tenement	iiijli xiijs iiijd.
Thomas Blokely, for a tenement	xxs.
Water Pooye, for a tenement	xls.
Summa	xvli xvjs viijd.
Summa de rentall	xxxvjli vjs.

Quyte Rent – off the which summa and landys paid to the Master of S. Bartholomu

Spetyll, for the quyte rent	xiijs iiijd.
Summa petet	

Obyte.

Also to iiij Wardeyns, the pece xld Summa	xiijs iiijd.
Also to pore men, goldsmythes, the pece xijd	xijs.
Also for the potacion on the even	xijs vjd.
Also for the denar for the Wardeyns and others on the morow	xvs vjd.
Summa	liijs iiijd.

Prystes

Also to Sir John Randull, his prist and scolemaster that syngeth for hym at Stokporte	xli.
Also to Sir John Bocley, his priste that syngeth for hym at Woodehed	iiijli vjs viijd.
Summa	xiiijli vjs viijd.
Summa totalis de bequestis	xvijli xiijs iiijd.

And they muste pray for the soules of Sir Edmund
Shaa and Dame Juliane his wif and Hugh their sonne

Hereafter foloweth the casuall vacacions, peticions, decrementys, reparacions, and other exspencys in the lawe, yff eny be in the yere, and of the clere rest of the seyd landys yerely:—

Reparacions – Also payed for reparacions done upon the seyd landys from the Xix day of Apryll the xij yere of Kyng Henry the vijth unto the same fest the xiij yere of the seyd Kyng as appereth by the Rentars' bokys. Summa xxs vjd.

Petycion – Also allowed in peticion frome the seyd day and yere to the seyd day and yere, as appereth by the Rentars' bokys.

Summa xiijs iiijd.

Costes in the Lawe – also payed in exspencys in the law from the seyd day and yere to the seyd day and yere, as appereth by the same bokys.

Summa lis iiijd.
Summa iiijli vs ijd.

And so remayneth clere to the Crafte, all paymentes and other charges deducted

Summa xiiijli vijs vjd.

Appendix 3

SOME APPOINTMENTS AND TRANSACTIONS OF SIR EDMOND SHAA, ILLUSTRATING THE MANNER OF HIS ENRICHMENT, ALSO A FEW OF SIR JOHN SHAA, HIS NEPHEW

(Unless otherwise stated the information is drawn from the Calendar of Patent Rolls, Edward IV, Richard III, and Henry VII; State Records.)

February 26, 1462. Westminster. 1 Edward IV.
Grant for life to Edmund Shaa, citizen and goldsmith of London from March 4 last of the office of sculptor of the King's dies for moneys and coinage of gold and silver to be coined within the Tower of London and England and the town of Calais, receiving the accustomed fees at the hands of the keeper of the exchange and mint, and all other accustomed profits.

March 28, 1475. 15 Edward IV.
Edmund Shaa, citizen and alderman (with three others) appointed to hear an appeal respecting a mercantile agreement.

June 18, 1480. 20 Edward IV.
Grant to Edmund Shaa, citizen and alderman and Thomas Montgomery, Kt., of the custody of lordships, manors, lands, etc., late of John Shawardyn, during the minority of John, their heir, and the custody and marriage of the latter.

April 26, 1482. 22 Edward IV.
Grant for life to John Shaa, citizen and goldsmith of London, from Easter last the office of graver of the King's irons for the King's mints and coinages of gold and silver within the Tower

of London, the realm of England and the town of Calais, receiving the accustomed fees etc. on surrender of the office by Edmund Shaa.

From Stow's *Survey of London*.

King Richard III called Sir Edmond Shaa 'his merchant'. Dec. 1, in 1st year, sold to him some of his plate, viz: – 4 Pots of silver parcel gilt, weighing 28 pounds 6 ounces, 3 Pots and 5 Bowls with a cover weighing 35 Pounds, 12 Dishes, 11 Sawcers Silver with gilt Borders, weighing 36 Pounds, 12 Plates silver with gilt Borders, weighing 44 Pounds 11 ounces. More, 2 Chargers, Silver with gilt Borders, 2 Charchers, 10 Sawcers, an Ewer parcel gilt, 4 Chargers, 2 with gilt Borders, 2 white. The weight of the said Plate was 275 Pounds, 4 ounces of Troy Weight, after 3*s*. 4*d*. the Ounce, came to £550:13:4. Which the King acknowledged to have received. (Above the receipt in Harl. MSS., 433, Brit. Museum.)

From Harleian MSS. 433 in the British Museum.

Warrant to pay to Sʳ Edmond Shawe, Knt. of London, Marchaunt, 200 markes for certen new yeres guifts bought of him ayenst the feste of Christy-messe in the 22 yr. of K. Edw. 4. Yeven at Westm. 5 feb. ano primo R. 3rd.

Warrant to Sʳ Edmonde Shaw, Knᵗ, to restore to the Abbot and Court of Malmesburie the remainder of their plate left in his Custodye by Sʳ Thos. St. Leger, Knt. to whom it was pawned and for which the said Abbot hath paid to the King a sum of money. Yeven at Westm. 9 Feb. ano primo R. 3rd.

August 8, 1483. 1 Richard III.

Commission de walliis et fossatis to the Bishop of Norwich (and many others, incl. Ed. Shaa) by the coast of the marsh of the Thames.

August 28, 1483. 1 Richard III.

Commission of Oyer and Terminer to Edmund Shaa, mayor (and others) in the city of London.

May 27, 1485. 2 Richard III.

Edmond Shaa (and three others) receive the Manor of South Wokyngton and other land which had been forfeited into the King's hands.

June 29, 1486. 1 Henry VII.

Grant to Reynold Bray, Kt., Edmond Shaa, Kt., and John Shaa, citizen and goldsmith of the wardship of the lands of John, son and heir of John Wrytell.

February 8, 1488. 3 Henry VII.

Licence to grant for ever the manor of Haunce, co. Bedford, to Reynold Bray, Edmund Shaa (and two others), Knts.

May 2, 1489. 4 Henry VII.

Grant to Reynold Bray, one of the Knights for the King's body, and John Shaa, for the keeping of the manors of Ramsey, Wrabnase, and Little Chisell, co. Essex, which have come into the king's hands.

November 28, 1491. 7 Henry VII.

Grant to John Shaa of the following goods and jewels, late of Robt. Mendrym, goldsmith, indicted of certain felonies: Six cups bound with silver gilt, 2 silver thuribles, one silver cross, one silver chalice, 2 silver goblets, 3 silver bowls, a bow and six arrows of silver, 5 gold rings with pearls, etc., etc.

February 26, 1492. 7 Henry VII.

Grant during the King's pleasure to John Shaa, King's servant, of the office of searcher in the port of London, with the half of all forfeitures seized by him and presented before the Barons of the Exchequer.

November 20, 1492. 8 Henry VII.

Indenture between the King and John Shaa and Bartholomew Reed, goldsmiths, to make moneys at the Mint in the Tower of London.

January 23, 1501. 16 Henry VII.

Grant during pleasure to John Shaa, Kt., of quit-rents and tenements in London, lately forfeited.

(Other references to John Shaa are numerous.)

Appendix 4

INQUISITIONES POST MORTEM OF SIR EDMOND SHAA, DAME JULIAN SHAA AND SIR JOHN SHAA
(State Records showing the family possessions.)

Sir Edmond Shaa.

Writ, 6 May 3 Henry VII. Inq. 4. Nov. 4. Henry VII.

By his will he directed that his feoffes should continue seised of such lands as he had purchased in fee simple, to the use of Julian his wife so long as unmarried, on conditions that she accepted the legacies given her by his will in full of that share of his goods to which she was entitled by the custom of London, and that immediately on her decease, or in case she disturbed his executors and sought a further share of his goods, she should have no part of his manors or lands, but that Hugh Shaa, his son, should have his manors of Arden Hall and Horndon House in tail male, with remainder to John Shaa, his cousin, in tail male, with remainder to his own right heirs.

He died 20 Apr. 3 Henry VII. Hugh Shaa aged 22 or more is his son and heir.

Essex. He died seised in fee of the
Manor of Horndon House, worth £14, and the Manor of Arden Hall, worth £10, held of William Poynes, as of the Manor of North Wokyndon, service unknown.

One Thomas Sanger and his wife, . . . acknowledged a fine on their lands to the said Edmond Shaa and one John Shaa, who survives, and the heirs of Edmond:
Twelve acres of land, four of marsh and a weir called 'le South Were' in Tyllyngham, worth 20/-, held of the Dean and Chapter of St. Paul's, by service of 2d.

One Reginald Rokes and others enfeoffed the said Edmond and one Thomas Wood and their heirs of:
All those lands and tenements in the Manor of Tyllyngham and a croft there called 'Gamys Croffte' worth 40/-, held of the Dean and Chapter of St. Paul's.

One Richard Herd of Tyllyngham and others enfeoffed the said Edmond, one Thomas Wode, and others, of
Lands called Hyfelds in Tyllyngham worth 26s 8d (24 acres) and other lands held of the Dean and Chapter.

One Thomas Wattes and others enfeoffed the said Edmund and John Shaa and their heirs of:
Lands, tenements etc. called Maundefeldes

and Dotes and Germeyns. Landes in Tyllyngham, worth 46/8d, held of the said Dean and Chapter by fealty and the rent of a red rose.

One John Keme, enfeoffed Edmund and John Shaa and their heirs of:
Lands in Westley and Langdon worth 41/-, held of the Abbot of Waltham, as of the Manor of Abbottes Hall in East Thorndon, service unknown.

One Andrew Newman enfeoffed Edmund and John Shaa and their heirs of:
The 'Fancroffte' worth 40/- in North Wokyngdon, service unknown.

The said Edmund Shaa died seised in fee of:
10 acres of land in Horndon and 2 messuages, 57 acres of land and 20/- rent in Horndon worth £3, held of the abbess of Barking, service unknown.

One John Courtman and his wife acknowledge a fine of the undermentioned lands to Edmund and John Shaa and their heirs:
A messuage, 60 acres land, 6 acres meadow, 5 acres wood and 15/- rent in Bulvan, worth £5, held of the said Abbess, service unknown.

One William Courtman enfeoffed Edmund and John Shaa and their heirs of:
Lands, tenements, rents and services in Bulvan, anciently called Shermans, worth £3, held of the Abbess by service of 1d.

One John Keme enfeoffed Edmond and John Shaa and their heirs of:
Lands etc. in Mokkyng called Fordmanys, Brokes, Brillis Croftes, Fordmannis Heth, worth 40/-, held of the said Abbess, service unknown.

One Thomas Porte enfeoffed Edmund and John Shaa and others to hold of the said Edmund and John in fee:
Lands, tenements, rents, services, sands, weirs, fisheries in Tyllyngham and Danngey, worth £3, formerly John Camside's, held of the said Dean and Chapter, service unknown.

Dame Julian Shaa, Widow

Writ 16 July 9 Henry VII. Inq. 29 Oct. 10 Henry VII.

Edmund Shaa, Knt, late her husband, being seised of the undermentioned manors of Horndon House and Arden Hall, enfeoffed John Shaa, Thomas Woode and others, thereof in fee to the use of his last will. By their permission and in accordance with the said will she occupied and took the issues and profits of the said manors during her life.

The said Edmund and John Shaa, Thomas Woode and other his co-feoffees being seised of lands in Tyllyngham, Daunsey, Westley, Langdon, Wokyngdon, Bulvan, and Mokkyng in fee, his survivors continue seised of the premises to the use of his last will; which was Julian to keep single, not to disturb etc. She to have the profits etc. with remainder to Hugh, his son, as touching the Manors of Horndon House and Arden Hall in tail male, with remainder to his cousin John Shaa, with remainder to his, the testator's, right heirs. She occupied all the said lands during her life and took the profits thereof. Julian took the profits of the land, marsh and weir at Tyllingham during her life, by permission of John Shaa, who after the death of Edmund was solely seised thereof, with reversion to Hugh Shaa as son and heir of Edmond, and after the death of the said Hugh issueless, with reversion to Margaret, now wife of Thomas Rich, and Katherine, now wife of William Brown, both mercers, as sisters of the said Hugh. She died 6 July last. The said Margaret aged 22 and more, and Katherine Brown, aged 20 or more, are her daughters and heirs.

Essex.
The Manors of Horndon House and Arden Hall worth £24, held of the king in chief by service of one knight's fee.

(Then follow the bulk of the estates previously mentioned in Sir Edmond's own I.P.M.)

John Shaa, Knight.
Inquisition last day of May, 19 Henry VII.
He died 26 Dec. 19 Henry VII. Edmund Shaa (12½ or more) is his son and heir.
John Shaa, by virture of an Act of Parliament 11 Henry VII as appears by letter patent of the same king was seised in fee tail of the undermentioned Manors, to him and his heirs male, with remainder in default to the right heirs of Edmund Shaa, Kt., deceased.

Manor of Ardern Hall, worth £13:6:8, held of the Mayor and Commonalty of London by service of fealty and a pair of gilt spurs if demanded, yearly, for all service.
Manor of Horndon House, worth £10, held of Henry Merney, Kt., held by service of fealty and a broad arrow, yearly, for all service. Long before his death he was seised of the following manors, etc:

10 messuages, 300 acres of land, 40 acres of wood in Halstead, held of Henry, Earl of Essex and the Prior of Colne. 2 messuages, 100 acres of land, 10 pasture, 10 meadow, 20 wood, in Southchirche. Manor and Advowson of Mochestanbrigge. 200 acres of land, 100 acres pasture, lately belonging to Reynold Bray, Kt. Manors of Barow Hall and Colmans, 300 acres land, 300 acres pasture, 100 acres meadow, 400 acres wood in Litill Barow, Colmans, Wakeryng Prytwell, Eastwood, Leigh, Rayleigh, and many other places. Manor of St. Laurence Hall, 100 acres land, 240 acres meadow, 100 acres pasture, 30 acres marsh, in St. Laurence Hall and Bradwell, etc., etc.
Inquisition, last day of May, 19 Henry VII.
More manors in Middlesex.
Manor of Oldford, co. Middlesex, 14 messuages, 14 gardens, 240 acres of land, 50 acres meadow, 80 acres pasture in Oldford, Stebenhith, Hakney, and Stratford atte Bowe.

By his will he directed *inter alia* that Margaret should have for life all his manors etc. in Oldford, Middlesex, with remainder after her decease to Edmund Shaa, his elder son, Reynold Shaa, his next son living, and Thomas Shaa, his younger son.

Appendix 5

To The Court of Assistants of the Worshipful Company of Goldsmiths.   19 October 1826.

In pursuance of the Instructions given to the Wardens for taking a view of the Grammar School at Stockport in Cheshire founded in the year 1506 (*sic*) by Sir Edmund Shaa, we the undersigned Wardens took advantage of the Summer Vacation as the most convenient and favourable opportunity for effecting that object and accordingly left London on the 20 August last, for the purpose of effecting our Mission.

We went by way of Chester, in order to our seeing the Bishop of the Diocese and conferring with his Lordship on the subject and obtaining his sentiments thereon, and we learned from his Lordship that the Master, the Rev. Elkanah Hoyle, was considered as being a very respectable though not an active man, that the Rector of the parish in which the School is situated is an intimate friend of the Master, and as such any opinion he might offer in reference to the general state and character of the School and Master should be received with some degree of caution.

His Lordship considered any alterations in the principles of the School inadvisable, whilst the present Master holds the appointment, but that on his death or retirement it would then become a serious consideration for the Company, and further, should they decide on the expediency of having Visitors, his Lordship would willingly be one and assist with his advice on any future occasions.

Having arrived at Stockport on Wednesday the 23 August, the Clerk to the Company was directed to address a letter to the Master requesting him to be at the Schoolhouse the following morning at 10 o'clock, thereby giving him notice of our arrival, but from its shortness precluding him from making special arrangements respecting the School. Mr. Prime Warden, accompanied by the Clerk, the same evening called on Mr. Prescot the Rector, and having informed him of the object of their visit he immediately entered upon the subject and spoke in unqualified terms of the Schoolmaster, and in answer to a question put to him regarding the stipend of the Master he stated that he received about £3:3:0 per annum for each boy. During the conversation Mr. Hoyle was announced, and being introduced we entered more fully into the subject, when Mr. Hoyle stated that he had hardly any free boys in the School, though admission had never been refused to any claiming to come in free, and from the remainder (between 40 and 50) he received £6:6:0 each per annum, sanctioned (he said) by the Corporation and the Inhabitants of Stockport upon his introducing a more enlarged scale of education than that required by the Founder, and a few other points they discussed as to the general character of the Town, in which there are many Cotton Manufactories of considerable importance, and very populous. We retired to meet again the following morning at the School, when Mr. Prescot said he would be present.

On Thursday, 24 August, we accordingly went to the School, where we met Mr. Hoyle, an assistant, and 42 boys, who appeared to be from the age of 8 to 14, very respectable and orderly in their conduct, evidently much above the class of the children of the poor, not much unlike the boys in Merchant Taylors School, the system of education pursued being somewhat similar, though inferior, from various causes, more particularly from the non-existence of Visitors, who of course tend to keep the Schoolmaster to his duty and the scholars more attentive to the instruction given them. The several classes were examined in our presence by the Rector and Master in Greek, Latin and English, embracing the following works, viz, Homer, Virgil, Ovid, the History of England and the customary Latin and Greek Grammars. The Junior Classes were either reading English books of minor importance, or writing or cyphering.

We (the Wardens) have much pleasure in stating that we found Mr. Hoyle's manners mild and affectionate, which was corroborated by the attachment evinced towards him on the part of the boys, and that the discipline and management of the School are creditable to Mr. Hoyle's exertions are proved by the fact (which he stated) that some of his pupils have been sent from him direct to College.

In reference to the state of the Building, which is situated in one of the public, though narrow, streets of the Town, we found it in a very dirty and dilapidated state, about 53 feet long, the School Room being about 42 feet long by 21 feet wide, fitted up with desks and forms, and over which there is another room of similar dimensions. The whole plot of ground as occupied for the purposes of the foundation is about 53 feet long by 43 wide, that part not used as a School Room being an enclosed yard or Forecourt, through which is the entrance to the Rooms. At the end of the building there is a convenience for the boys overhanging a wide ditch, which from its stagnant state is very offensive, close to which there is an old manufactory unoccupied.

Having completed our visit to the School we went to the New Church of St. Mary, a fine structure, where there are six pews in the Gallery, to the right and left of the Organ, Nos. 1, 2, 3, 34,

35, 36 allotted to the School, the expense of £54 at which they were finished not having been paid, they are not yet considered as the Company's property. How such an expense was incurred or whether any intimation of the alterations had ever been sent up for the information of the Company, we could not learn, but we desired Mr. Hoyle to furnish the particulars for our information, and also of some repairs he had at times done to the School.

We subjoin a list of the Scholars at present in the School, as they stand in the classes, with the business or profession (if any) in which their parents are engaged and their places of residence, the result of which strongly confirms the information we obtained as regards the non-attendance of free boys, arising from a reluctance of their parents to send them, so long as they can find employment in the Mills and other branches of Manufacture, which they do from seven years and upwards.

Having laid before you an account of our proceedings, we beg to submit for consideration an opinion first in regard to the School Building, that a survey should be immediately taken and an estimate obtained of all the necessary repairs it may require to render it more convenient for the purposes of instruction.

As regards the Master and the internal regulations of the School, we see no reason for believing that there has been any defection on his part with respect to its management, though we conceived he has held out no encouragement for the admission of free boys. And we fear (from indirect information obtained) that such of the boys as enter free are made to do the drudgery of the School, such as cleaning it out and lighting the fire, thus causing them to be looked upon with a feeling of contempt and thereby injurious to the good discipline of the School. It probably may account in part for there being only 3 free boys within its walls. We are therefore inclined to believe that were the School established upon different principles to those by which it is at present regulated the benefit to the children in the Neighbourhood would be much greater, particularly when it is recollected that the Master, by the Will of the Founder is required 'freely without salary taking of any person (except only the salary specified in this Will) to teach all manner of persons children and others that will come to him to learn, as well in the Town of Stockport and other parishes thereabouts, the Science of Grammar until they be instructed therein unto their capacities'.

Whilst the present Master retains the appointment we do not recommend any alteration being attempted (except that to which we have just alluded), nor do we think any addition necessary to the stipend of the Master, whose income (exclusive of other sources) amounts, we are informed, to £280 per annum, to which may be added (should you defray the expense before referred to of erecting the Pews) such sum as might be obtained by letting of the same, which the Master benefited by in the Old Church. Looking forward, nevertheless, to the appointment of another Master, which will in the course of time occupy the attention of the Company, as Patrons of the School, we recommend that serious consideration be then given to the matter, both as regards the situation in life and character of the person to be appointed and the Salary to be paid him, which should be so far increased as to make it imperative on him to instruct gratuitously a certain number of children in Reading, Writing and Arithmetic.

Referring to the expenses incurred in the Church, and such as may have been occasioned by the Master for repairs he has done to the School, and in justice to the good character Mr. Hoyle has supported during the time he has held the appointment, we cannot conclude our report without recommending to your consideration the propriety of repaying such sums as he may have thus expended, and also that the sum of £54 or such other sum as may be found due, be paid into the hands of the Treasurer of the Building Fund for the new Church, so as to redeem the six Pews and thereby make them the property of the Company.

John Garratt, Prime Warden.
Edmund Waller Rundell
Samuel Haynes.

Appendix 6

from the 1826 Report

BOYS BELONGING TO THE FREE GRAMMAR SCHOOL OF STOCKPORT

Boys' Names	Profession or Trade of Parents	Residence
First Class:		
Killer	Surgeon, etc.	Stockport
Worthington	Tradesman: wealthy	Stockport
Vaughan	Tradesman	Stockport
Second Class:		
Fern, Senr.	Opulent	Stockport
Fern, Junr.	Opulent	Stockport
Third Class:		
Jepson	Solicitor: wealthy	Heaton Norris
Whitelegg	A private gentleman	Northenden
Knowles	Tradesman: wealthy	Stockport
Bowring	Wealthy Brewer	Stockport
Fourth Class:		
Garside, Grandson to	Tradesman: opulent	Stockport
Clayton	A Respectable Solicitor	Stockport
Paulden	A Respectable Solicitor	Stockport
Walmsley	Wealthy Tradesman	Stockport
Young, nephew to	Gentleman of Landed property	Bramhall
Ashton	Respectable Tradesman	Stockport
Fifth Class:		
Rawes	Eminent Physician	Stockport
Partington	Of considerable property	Stockport
Worthington, Junr.	Wealthy Tradesman	Stockport
Wilkinson	Wealthy Tradesman	Stockport
Broadhurst	Wealthy Tradesman	Stockport
Turner	Wealthy Wine Merchant	Stockport
Walker	Respectable Brewer	Stockport
Sixth Class:		
Andrew	Gentleman of Wealth	4 miles distant
Ainsworth	Respectable Tradesman	Macclesfield
Potter	Respectable Tradesman	Stockport
Bowring, Junr.	Wealthy Brewer	Stockport
Broadhurst	Respectable Mercer	Stockport
North	Respectable Tradesman	Stockport
Lingard	Eminent Solicitor	Stockport
Clayton	Eminent Solicitor	Stockport
Whitlegg, Junr.	Private Gentleman	Northenden
Knight	Respectable Tradesman	Stockport
Bostock	Of good Landed Property	2 miles distant
Seventh Class:		
Ferns, Tertius	Opulent Tradesman	Stockport
Vaughan	Eminent Solictor	Stockport
Walmsley	Respectable Solicitor	Marple
Wilkinson	Respectable Tradesman	Stockport
Kinder	Father deceased, family respectable	Stockport
Broadhurst	Respectable Tradesman	Stockport
Eighth Class:		
Robinson	Respectable Tradesman	Stockport
Pickford	Respectable Tradesman	Stockport
Ninth Class:		
Drabble	Brewer	In the Country
Hampson	Hatter	Stockport
Tenth Class:		
Broadhurst, Junr.	Mercer	Stockport
Vaughan	Eminent Solicitor	Stockport
Foster	Grandfather wealthy	Stockport
Eleventh Class:		
Walmsley	Eminent Solicitor	Marple
Pickford	Respectable Tradesman	Stockport
Birch	Sheriff's Officer	Stockport

114

NOTES AND BIBLIOGRAPHY

Dates

Until the middle of the eighteenth century, the New Year in England fell on 25th March, Lady Day, the Feast of the Annunciation of the Blessed Virgin Mary. Thus, when Sir Edmond dated his will 'the xxthe day of the Monthe of Marche the yere of our Lorde after thaccompte of the Churche of Englond Mcccclxxxvijth' [1487], he was referring to the year which we should now regard as 1488. All dates in this book have been converted into our present system of reckoning, but it should be borne in mind that a reference dated by us to between 1st January and 24th March of any year prior to 1752 will be a year later than the date to which it was regarded as belonging at the time. The 1751 'Act for Regulating the Commencement of the Year; and for Correcting the Calendar Now in Use' also changed England from the use of the Julian to the Gregorian Calendars, by that time eleven days out of line. The Act decreed that 1752 should start on 1st January, and also that September should lose eleven days, with the 14th following immediately on the 2nd. So as not to lose eleven days' taxes, the predecessors of the Inland Revenue added the days to Lady Day, and commenced the tax year on April 6th – a custom still with us today.

Money

Until 15th February 1971, the £ was divided into twenty shillings, and each shilling into twelve pennies or pence (£ s d). Since then, the £ has been divided into 100 new pence (£ p). Thus, ten shillings is the equivalent of 50 new pence. A marc or mark was worth 13s 4d (about 67p).

Particular Sources

For the story of Stockport Grammar School up to 1860, the primary sources are the Court Minute Books, the Committee Minute Books, and the Wardens' Accounts of the Worshipful Company of Goldsmiths; from 1860 to the present day these continue to contain references to the School, but because of the break in 1860 do not, and cannot, tell the full story. These sources are complemented and supplemented by additional boxed archive material at the Goldsmiths' Hall, under the reference RIII.

For the Stockport High School, 1857–1860, the Governors' Minute Books are preserved at Stockport Grammar School.

For the period 1860 to the present day, the primary sources are the Governors' Minutes Books and Account Books preserved at Stockport Grammar School. A 'public' view of events is provided by *The Stockport Grammar School Magazine* (1898–1902) and *The Stopfordian* (1929–date); and also by the *Stockport Advertiser* (1822–1981), the *Stockport Express* (1889–1981), and the *Stockport Express Advertiser* (1981–date).

General Sources

More up-to-date books are listed below. This is only a selection of the literature available, dealing with Stockport or its Grammar School either specifically or generally. The dates given are of the latest printing of the edition consulted.

Baines, E., *History, Directory, & Gazetteer of the County Palatine of Lancaster, 1825*, 1968

Bardsley, C., *Secondary Education in Stockport, 1902–1944*, University of Manchester M. Ed., 1963

Barlow, T. E., Hadfield, B., & Gosling, J. G., *Stockport Sunday School Bi-Centenary*, 1984

Beck, J., *Tudor Cheshire*, 1969

Bu'Lock, J. D., *Pre-Conquest Cheshire, 383–1066*, 1972

Chadwick, B., *Educational Provision in the Hundred of Macclesfield during the 19th Century*, University of Manchester M. Ed., 1967

Christie-Miller, J. A., *Stockport and the Stockport Advertiser*, 1972

Colclough, W. J., *The Story of Stockport School*, 1986

Dodd, A. E. & E. M., *Peakland Roads and Trackways*, 1980

Dore, R. N., *The Civil Wars in Cheshire*, 1966

Driver, J. T., *Cheshire in the Later Middle Ages*, 1971

Fowler, J. C., *Development of Elementary Education in Chester, 1800–1902*, University of Liverpool M.A., 1968

Galvin, F., Lees, B., & Porter, G., *From the Ground Upwards: Stockport through its Buildings*, 1982

Harris, B. E., *A History of the County of Chester*, Vol. 2, 1979 & Vol. 3, 1980, ('The Victoria County History')

Hewitt, J. H., *Cheshire under the Three Edwards*, 1967

Horn, T., *The School in the Sixties*, 1966

Hurst, J., *The Old Stockport Grammar Schools*, 1921

Hodson, J. H., *Cheshire, 1660–1780*, 1978

Husain, B. M. C., *Cheshire Under the Norman Earls*, 1973

Pevsner, N. & Hubbard, E., *The Buildings of England: Cheshire*, 1971

Phillips, C. B., & Smith, J. H., *Stockport Probate Records, 1578–1619*, 1985

Reddaway, T. F., & Walker, L. E. M., *The Early History of the Goldsmiths' Company*, 1975

Robson, D., *Some Aspects of Education in Cheshire in the 18th Century*, Chetham Society, 3rd series, no. 13

Scard, G., *Cheshire, 1760–1900*, 1981

Schofield, E. M., *Some Aspects of the Endowed Schools Act 1869 with particular reference to Stockport Grammar School*, 1975

Short, D., *Science Education in Stockport, 1860–1918*, University of Manchester M. Ed., 1978

Thompson, F. H., *Roman Cheshire*, 1965

Varley, W. J., *Cheshire before the Romans*, 1964

Further reading is indicated on pp 326–337 of Varley, B., *The History of Stockport Grammar School*, 1957.

It should be clearly noted that the chapter references and notes which follow are *additional* to the notes and references contained in Varley.

Chapter references and notes

Stockport

1   There is no detailed modern History of Stockport. The geography and early history of the town are briefly covered in the Cheshire Community Council works and the Victoria County History noted above. Other works, of more than mere antiquarian interest despite their age are the volumes by Earwaker, Ormerod, and Heginbotham mentioned by Varley.

Shaa

1   For further details on the various branches of the family, including Sir Edmond's descendants, see Varley, B., op. cit., pp 1–48.

2   For Shaa as a goldsmith, see Reddaway & Walker, op. cit., pp 176–177, 306–307, and references there.

3   For Shaa's royal commissions, The Calendars of Patent Rolls covering the reigns of Edward IV, Richard III, and Henry VII, and British Museum Harleian MS 433, should be consulted (Extracts are printed below in Appendix 3).

4   See below, Appendix 1.

School and Chapel

1   After the Reformation, the Chapel is not mentioned until the 19th century – see p 43. The reference to 1846 was the earliest which Prideaux could find in response to a query at the end of the 19th century.

2   The 12s 0d continued to be paid out to the poor even after 1548 (eg, Wardens' Accounts and Court Books, K, p 46).

3   Goldsmiths' Archives, R III, 217 & 218, f11.

4   According to the Watson ms (Varley, B. op. cit., p 57) the salary was forfeit to the Crown; the case appeared in the Court of Exchequer in 1559 (Wardens' Accounts & Court Books K, p 92). The transfer to Gardner was effected before 1712 (R III, 2).

The Sixteenth Century

1   The Latin of De Profundis is printed on p 74. It is an apt psalm, especially in view of the horrors of the Wars of the Roses. The English of the King James Bible runs as follows;

'Out of the depths have I cried unto thee, O Lord.

Lord, hear my voice: let thine ears be attentive to the voice of my supplications.

If thou, Lord, shouldest mark iniquities, O Lord, who shall stand?

But there is forgiveness with thee, that thou mayest be feared.

I wait for the Lord, my soul doth wait, and in his word do I hope.

My soul waiteth for the Lord more than they that watch for the morning: I say, more than they that watch for the morning.

Let Israel hope in the Lord: for with the Lord there is mercy, and with him plenteous redemption.

And he shall redeem Israel from all his iniquities.'

2   RIII, 2a, s.v. Read, 1505. Despite the great changes which were to occur in English religion and society, these observances were not officially replaced until the 1820s (R III, 170, 26 September 1827).

3   An Acte for dissolucõn of Colledges, 37 Henry VIII, c4.

4   The exemptions included, for example, First fruits and Tenths (27 Henry VIII, c42) and Subsidies (34, 35 Henry VIII, c24). The requirement dated from 3rd August 1547 (*Tudor Royal Proclamations*, 1964, p 289).

5   How regularly this was done remains unclear. Certainly as late as 1771 the procedure was for the Company to 'nominate, elect, & admit' the Master and then 'humbly to beseech' the Bishop to grant him a licence. See also R III, 91, [Fox's Charity] and Court Books 15, f351 (1752) and 19, 368.

6   Certainly the survival of the School was a matter about which even the Goldsmiths themselves were unclear, and as late as the 19th century

they had recourse to Counsel to help them to understand the situation. His opinion was that there was a 'conclusive presumption' that the Company ought to pay the annual £10 to the School: that is, the Company had never failed to pay the money, and it was therefore presumed that it should be paid – but no one knew why. (R III, 199; according to R III, 217, 'no claim . . . is known to have been at any time made', but cf. Varley, B., op. cit., p 57 (= Bodleian Library MS Top Cheshire, B1, p 139).)

7 Calendar of Patent Rolls III, 4th July 1550, pp 388/9 and IV, 13th August 1551, p 134; Wardens' Accounts I f29, 17th January 1548. £1 13 4d was paid for the anniversary of Sir Bartholomew Read, probably made up of £1 to the poor of the parish and 13 4d to the Wardens, which was still paid at the preaching of an annual sermon as late as 1822; see also Appendix. Varley, B., op. cit., p 57 n8 is probably derived, via Prideaux I, p 55, from R III, 200.

The Seventeenth Century

1 Early in this century the Goldsmiths were still suffering from their dues to the Crown (Varley, B., op. cit., p 57 perhaps = Patent 17 James I, 24th July 1619; Act for the general quiet of the Subject against all pretences of Concealment, 1623), but their financial state was by no means disastrous. From a rent roll of 1610 (R III, 2316) it appears that large fines, amounting to £700 and upwards, were received in respect of property, excluding that in Wood Street which was mixed up with other property, but a small portion of which was let for £12 p.a. and a fine of £20.

2 There was also a tradition that he had gone to school in Congleton (Bodleian Library, MS Top Cheshire, B1, p 123), not mentioned in DNB.

The Eighteenth Century

1 Dale's ability and constant service were eloquently recorded by the Company (Court Book 16, f6 [25th April 1754]).

Hoyle

1 Hoyle, born in 1767, was admitted to Pembroke College in 1786, ordained in 1790, and readmitted to Pembroke as a pensioner in 1795. He is referred to variously as MA and LLB, but the university records do not mention his taking any degree.

2 See Appendices 5 and 6.

3 The details concerning the new School are in Court Books 24 & 25, Committee 18, R III 196-8a.

Greek Street

1 The land surveyor was also from Warrington, one Henry Hobden (R III, 196).

2 Hardwick had his drawings for the new School bound in a volume, which was presented to the Goldsmiths on 15th December 1837 (Court Book 27, p 45). He continued as the Company's Architect and Surveyor until he was obliged to resign 'in consequence of his age and infirmities' after 39 years' of service on 29th January 1868 (Court Book 32, p 413).

Middleton

1 The Goldsmiths were certainly taking a very close interest in all aspects of the School, in ways of which Sir Edmond could have been proud. In 1834 they declined to honour Middleton's request to create a fourth Latin class, since such an increase may 'by degrees tend to exclude from the School those Boys whose . . . education [was] more consonant with the intentions of the original founder of the school'. (Court Book 26, p 175).

Gurney

1 Gurney reported, without any comment, that the boys had left in his monthly report of 26th August 1850 (R III, 207).

2 Gurney's £50 rise was granted both because he was so busy and also because he had only two boarders in his house. (Court Book 29, p 372).

3 In January 1854 any further reorganization had been ruled out 'until Gurney leaves' (Committee Book 21, p 1).

4 Counsel's opinion had been already taken in May 1847 on the Goldsmiths' obligations arising from Sir Edmond's will (R III, 200).

The Break

1 The School figures in the Goldsmiths' archive only intermittently from March 1860 (R III 210–222A), and the Governors' Minute Books held at School tell the story from now on. Corroboration for statements made in the text will not be referred to in these notes, as it will be found in the Minutes for the Meeting next following the event. Mr. William Johnston, Clerk to the Governors from 1898 to 1942, alleged that the School's own early records were deliberately burnt in 1860 after the Goldsmiths withdrew. Certainly the only pre-1860 documents at School are the Schole and Poor Book from 17th October 1693 to 18th October 1778, Coppock's High School Minutes for 1857–1860, detailing the meetings of 1858 and 1859, and the Admissions Register from 1832.

2 From 1864 onwards the Minute Books regularly record various schemes from Hamilton for making ends meet.

3 The Examiner, the Rev. H. Cottam, also suggested that in future his report should not be read out: 'I think that the Trustees and the Headmaster might make more use of the examiner's judgement and advice if the report were not published. In saying this I do not in the least intend you to infer that I have anything to suggest that I would not like the general public to know. But, I can quite see that an occasion might occur on which it would be desirable that the examiner's report should be regarded as the advice of an independent adviser to the Trustees and Headmaster and not intended for the public'. It was not until Daniels's time that this advice was heeded (see p 58).

4 There was also a discussion on whether the School was to be lit by gas – but no decision was reached.

Nadir and Rebirth

1 The Staff in December 1890 were Rev. W. A. Pemberton (Headmaster), Rev. P. J. D. Johnson, Messrs C. H. Raven, R. J. Escreet, J. Russell, M. Cossart, W. Sidebotham, C. J. Smith, and Sgt. Sash.

Daniels

1 A 'Motor Generator' was purchased for £50 in 1906 to 'study electricity and its modern developments'.

2 Mr. and Mrs. Daniels retired to Leicester; he died on 17th February 1946.

Gilkes

1 Gilkes was the third son of the Rev. A. H. Gilkes, Master of Dulwich College from 1885 to 1914.

2 South had taken his first school party to the Lake District at Easter 1909.

3 *The Stopfordian* from 1929 provides many incidental details in these pages from now on. Detailed references are not given in these notes, but confirmation may be sought in the issue of the magazine next following the event.

4 Teachers' salaries were also cut by 10% by the National Economy (Education) Order in 1931. The cut was restored in December 1933.

5 These works cost £1,680!

6 For Sir Edmond as Mayor of London, see p 101.

Philpot

1 South had been the School's first official 'Second Master', reappointed annually from 1918.

2 For an English translation, see p 116.

3 A portrait of Varley now hangs in the Hallam Library.

Scott

1 The decision to abolish Saturday morning school aroused strong passions on both sides. Whatever the social, educational, and political considerations were – Saturday was the one day when the buses were comparatively empty!

2 Buying the same site in 1909 would have cost £11,000.

Wright

1 Mrs. Renshaw had originally been appointed in 1974.

Bird

1 'He who endures, conquers.'

INDEX

Homer, 112
Honorius, Emperor, 12
Horn, Theodore, 76, 78, 94, 98
Horndon, 106, 110
    House, 110, 111
Horne, Sir William, 15
House of Lords, 48
Howell, C. F., 44, 46
    Ruth, 46
Hoyle, Rev. Elkanah, 30f, 40, 112f
Hugo, Victor, 89
Hulton, Sir Randall, 21
Humphreys, Capt., 41
Hyde, F. O. Charles, 74
Hymers College, Hull, 80

Industrial Fund, 77
Ingoldesthorpe, Lady Joan, 16
Inquisitions PM, 110, 111
International School of Mountaineering, 95
Ipswich School, 30
Irish Society, 32
Isherwood, John, 41
Itinerant, The, 30
Ives, Lister, 53

Jackson, Rev. William, 28f
Jacobites, 27
John, Sir (the priest), 107
Johnson, Thomas, 26
Johnston, Albert, 63, 84, 95
    Eleanor, 84
    J. W., 54
    W., 62
    W. S., 67, 78, 89

Kay, Samuel, 62, 65
Kelk, Sister, 107
Keme, John, 110
Kensall Green Cemetery, 31
Kershaw, James, 45
    W. A., 87, 91, 94
King George V School, Southport, 67
King's School, Chester, 20
King's School, Macclesfield, 20, 22, 23, 26
Kingswood School, Bath, 94
King William's College, 41
Kirkby Lonsdale, 76
Kirke, Mr., 24
Knight, Ald. W. C., 82, 86, 97
Knowles, Rev. J. C., 29

Lamb, Sir Horace, 56, 62, 68
Lancashire County Council, 56
Lang, Mr., 24
Langdon, 110, 111

Lee, Right Rev. Dr. James Prince, 48
    John, 21
Leech, Daniel, 26
Legh, Sir Peter, 24
    Sir Urian, 24, 25
Leigh, James, 51, 52, 56
    Thomas, 23
Lesotho, 88
Lichfield, Diocese of, 22
Lily's Grammar, 20
Lingard, William, 24
Little Chisell, 109
Livery Companies, 22
Lloyd, Isaac, 21
Lloyd's of London, 32
London 16
    & Birmingham Railway Co., 43
    & North Western Railway Co., 59
    Mayor of, 14, 104, 111
    Raffe, 108
    Sheriff of, 14
    Tower of, 14, 108, 109
    University, 51
Londonderry, 32
Long, see Lang
Longdendale, see Mottram in Longdendale
Losli, Seti, 92
Lovelock, J. D., 96
Lowe, Alexander, 23, 27, 101
    Francis, 23
    John, 23
Lowys, 14
Ludlow Castle, 14
Lupus, Hugh, 12

Macclesfield, 27
    School, 20, 22, 23, 26
Magna Carta, 56
Mallory & Irvine, 95
Malmesbury, Abbot of, 109
    Bishop of, 95
Manchester, 12
    & Birmingham Railway Co., 43
    & Liverpool District Banking Co., 21
    Art Gallery, 72
    Bishop of, 48
    Grammar School, 20, 29, 40, 53, 59, 71
    Guardian, 84
    Sheffield & Lincolnshire Railway Co., 16
    University, 56, 67
Market Bosworth, 15
Marple, 25
    Hall, 41
Marsland, J., 43
    P. E., 43
Mason, Luke, 25
Medd, Peter, 46

Typeset and printed by Heffers Printers Limited, Cambridge